QUEST FOR QUALITY

QUEST FOR QUALITY

Ian Webb

The Industrial Society

First published 1991 by
The Industrial Society
Robert Hyde House
48 Bryanston Square
London W1H 7LN
Tel 071 262 2401

© *Ian Webb, 1991*

ISBN 0 85290 683 8

A CIP catalogue record for
this book is available
from the British Library.

Design and production in association with
Book Production Consultants
47 Norfolk Street, Cambridge CB1 2LE
Typeset by Witwell Ltd, Southport
Printed and bound in Great Britain by Bookcraft (Bath) Ltd, Midsomer Norton, Avon

CONTENTS

Preface

I was a late convert to thinking of quality as a separate subject. This was not through any aversion to quality; far from it, but rather, it appeared to be used as a management label for activities which could stand on their own merits. Charles Handy made the point years ago that organisational people tend to interpret issues with their own disciplines and this was certainly so with some views on quality. To this day, it is possible to find the subject portrayed as principally a matter of statistics and quantitative methods, or of design, or of marketing, of operations and inventory control, of supplier relations, or of personnel and motivation. Of course, all of these topics have long been established as separate subjects and introducing quality can even be a source of confusion. Take a reading list on quality after all; one work is on just in time, another on marketing, another on design and many more, most of them giving the impression that theirs is the best route to perfection. So why not leave the design to the designers, the people issues to the personnel department, the marketing to the marketers and so on? That, at any rate was the view I took for several years.

And yet there often seemed to be shortcomings with the way business used to be conducted. A conventional corporate appraisal, for example, of a 'get all the facts, run the numbers and draw the conclusions' variety was quite evidently unsuited to handling several questions, among them quality. Major corporations, widely seen as progressive, sometimes failed to address quality at all at Head Office.

Instead, they were run through plans, budgets and variances and the promotion fast track was filled with those who were bright with the figures. Even the first rumblings of competition from Japan were widely misunderstood. Somehow, those who were adept at management through financial control, almost without exception, had never been trained to look for quality. No, quality was an issue to be decentralised to the works, where its implementation was principally through an army of inspectors.

Rising competition from the Far East and less protection for the UK market within Europe were to force the change; quality just had to be improved. However, many of the first efforts led to disappointing results. Numerous attempts to introduce quality circles, new systems for operations control, marketing drives and many more, often seemed to make little difference when the results were judged either against the overall quality problem, or against the rising quality standards from the competition. Instead of such faltering, piecemeal steps, what really worked was a comprehensive approach. Substantial quality improvement thus involved getting several disciplines together and uniting the workforce. And because it worked that way, quality could be justified as a separate subject.

In writing a book, there is a huge debt to so many people, most of whom go unsung. However, this one could not have appeared in its present form without the great help given to me on many topics and organisations. So my thanks go to, Ministry of Defence sources, to D. G. 'Spike' Spickernell, to R. M. McKinlay of British Aerospace, Tony Lewis of Ford Motor Company, John Poppleton and Graham Godwin of Marks and Spencer, Angus Stirling and Ivor Blomfield of The National Trust, Count Numa Labinsky and his Board at Nimbus Records, John Makepeace and John Eden of the Parnham Trust, M. J. Mann of BSI, Diane Smith of the Design Council, Peter Gorb of the London Business School and David Lobley of NEDO. In varying ways, they practice or represent some of the best of British quality. Lastly I must thank the staff of the Industrial Society Press who have ensured I was never quite working alone. In particular, I must mention the three who have supported, encouraged and edited in such a positive manner: Nick Brealey, Gilles Desmons and Chris Shaw. I am most grateful to all of them.   Ian Webb.

1

What is quality?

THE CUSTOMER'S POINT OF VIEW

We all believe that we can recognise quality – or the lack of it – in the many different products and services we buy or use as ordinary consumers. But defining quality is quite another matter. Part of the problem is that a number of different attributes may give a product or service the impression of quality. For example, fine craftsmanship and finish, or a design which enables the product to do what it is intended to do outstandingly well, will give a product or service an aura of quality, as will its availability, rapid delivery and the service provided by its supplier. All of these factors and more may register 'quality' in the eye of the customer, especially if a product has several quality attributes: a bad performance on any one of them detracts from the positive impression of the others.

Although customers often see quality in absolute terms – the product either has quality or it has not – usually this assessment is a subjective one. Perceptions of quality differ and so consensus may be hard to achieve. Because any group of consumers will display differing views of quality, it becomes possible to talk of the degree of quality in a product or service when considering the market as a whole.

Furthermore, individual views may alter over time. A product considered advanced at the time of purchase may be regarded as a museum piece a generation later. Its aura of quality faded as its technology became obsolete. Exactly when the item stopped having quality is hard to establish.

Quality, to the customer, is determined by the degree to which the product satisfies the needs for which it was acquired. Sometimes the notion of quality is associated so closely with another term, 'reliability', that the two appear to be interchangeable. The distinction between them principally concerns the time factor. 'Reliability' implies the performance of an intended function for a long time after purchase, without interruption. It is often abbreviated to quality over time, subject to technological obsolescence.

THE PRODUCER'S POINT OF VIEW

The customer's product-related view of quality is essentially the same as the producer's, but from a different perspective and this introduces several complications. Producers have to establish what their customers' needs are and then attempt to meet them as closely as possible. The extent to which producers succeed in this market-based approach determines whether or not they develop quality products.

This concept of quality, expressed in terms of the simple principle of meeting customer expectations, is the basis of the most frequently used definitions of the term 'quality'. In any case, it is difficult to envisage producers who do not consider that market orientation and concern for their customers' needs are a major part of their strategy.

However, there are situations when straightforward market orientation alone is insufficient to describe the nature of quality. Part of the problem arises from pricing policies. With many items (possibly most) quality is partly evaluated in relation to a given price level. If prices are raised perceived quality falls, and *vice versa*. It is easy to accommodate prices by qualifying our definition so that it reflects the customer's expectations of quality at that price level; but, if 'quality' can be manipulated in this way, the concept becomes limited.

THE EFFECTS OF MARKET IMPERFECTIONS

As the impression of quality is not determined solely by price, market-related definitions alone cannot adequately describe it. Besides, developing quality through market orientation presupposes that markets give accurate signals to producers about customers' preferences. This may be substantially true for many products, but the exceptions have probably become more important in recent years.

Part of the difficulty is that some customer requirements are incompletely expressed through the market. For example, both supply patterns and apparent preferences may be distorted by the fact that the marketplace is so dominated by one supplier that there are no alternatives to its product. Of course, the art of running an organisation may extend to taking an inspired guess and supplying markets with what they really do need, despite all the confusing information. So the market-orientated definition of 'quality' may need changing to be not what the customers' needs are but what the producers think they are.

Cases where some or all of the likes and dislikes of customers cannot be expressed through the market are even harder to handle. Sometimes these needs are described in the economic terms 'externalities' and 'collective good components'. These two pieces of jargon mean, in effect, that satisfying an immediate customer demand can be at variance with the welfare of society as a whole. A few years ago it might have seemed valid to argue that such questions were a problem not for trading organisations but rather for the public sector and charitable institutions. Paying taxes and contributing to charities were seen as discharging businesses' responsibility. However, this attitude has changed. In Japan, G. Taguchi has come up with a definition of quality which takes account of society's welfare, as well as of the interests of the purchaser. In effect, as the world becomes more crowded with people, goods and pollution, the pursuit of quality requires producers to heed all the consequences of their products, both initially and over time. Today, the emergence of Green issues in

Europe provides enough cause for manufacturers to re-examine the wider impact of their activities.

PRODUCT ORIENTATION IN PRACTICE

In spite of the strong arguments for market orientation, producers often have to confront an array of technical issues which condition products. In fact, it is possible for some of these to become so important to the development of quality that quality becomes identified within the organisation in terms of the discipline or technique concerned. Among the factors against which quality may be judged are marketing, industrial design, engineering design, the working of operations, process control and customer service. Any of these, under the right circumstances, can become crucial to notions of quality. It can even seem that quality is *entirely* a matter of process control, customer service, or any one of the other factors. So, not surprisingly, product-orientated definitions of 'quality' are often expressed in terms of, for example, 'conformance to specification'.

Several of the major books on quality have been written by people with a great concern for getting something done to improve quality within organisations. The Raby Committee report, which advocates the use of quality assurance in military procurement, is an example. P. B. Crosby, associated with many major quality programmes, uses 'conformance to requirements' within a product-related context, though clearly some of these requirements may themselves be market-related.

QUALITY IN SERVICE ORGANISATIONS

When possible case studies for this book were being researched, examples of quality in service organisations were much harder to find than among manufacturers. This might seem surprising, as the relative importance of services within the national economy has risen for many years and the overseas trading performance of UK services has been strong. There is also a preponderance of service companies among small-business start-ups. Not necessarily conclusive in themselves, such points do lend weight to the instinctive impression that quality ought to be more readily apparent within the services sector.

The main reason why this is not the case is simple. Quality is harder to see in a service organisation because it is harder to define it than in manufacturing where precise measures can be related to such factors as specifications, reliability and design.

One reason why a simple market-orientated definition of the term 'quality' has attracted little criticism in the past is that nearly everything produced on the subject has been written from the standpoint of manufacturing. True, few works entirely omit discussion of services, but, even where the coverage is considerable, for the most part the discussion is centred on manufacturing industry.

Service organisations tend to face greater problems with concealed demand and with the failure of the market mechanism to express completely who the customers are and what they want. This is particularly true of services in the public sector.

DECIDING A DEFINITION

Selecting a definition of the term 'quality', is at the heart of deciding what it constitutes in a particular organisation. Although there are situations where this is straightforward and a clear choice is possible, more commonly several purposes have to be met. One solution is to use multiple definitions after the example of W. A. Shewhart in his *Economic Control of Quality of Manufactured Product* (1931). Shewhart first defines quality as the 'goodness' of a product, a term he derives from Aristotle, and then follows it up with definitions for product-orientated and statistical quality.

J. M. Juran and F. A. Gryna, in the 4th edition of *Juran's Quality Control Handbook* (1988), likewise manage to cover virtually any purpose by using a general and essentially market-orientated definition of quality: 'fitness for purpose or use'. Users are then encouraged to establish quality objectives for whatever matters to them, and in this way the definition is turned into an open-ended list of topics

5

covering anything from engineering and the market to the organisation's history and traditions.

However, more important than agreeing on a precise definition is deciding what makes up quality. For this, some of the points to consider usually include:

- Customer need expressed through the market
- Concealed market requirements
- The role of pricing
- Product or service design and specification
- Conformance to specification, now and over time

2

Quality through operations control and quantitative methods

STATISTICAL PROCESS CONTROL

Until the rise of large-scale manufacture, responsibility for quality control rested with those engaged in the production process: craft skills, standards and traditions may have been organised and determined by others, sometimes away from the place of work, but the operatives themselves were at least partly responsible for the implementation. This pattern began to break down with the introduction of the division of labour, and change was hastened by the onset of flowline working. Responsibility and authority for maintaining quality were now separated from the operatives. A new function – called 'quality control' – was introduced and this was carried out through inspection of the final product.

Such a system failed to produce suitable results in many applications. In the 1920s several people started independently to look afresh at production processes, to analyse them, understand them and then correct them in an effort to raise product quality. Among these people were Dr Dudding at the General Electric Company, working on lightbulbs, L. H. C. Tippett of the British Cotton Industry Research Association, working on textiles, and Dr W. A. Shewhart of Bell Telephone Laboratory in the US, working on telecommunication components. The tool they used for the analysis and correction of processes is known as Statistical Process Control, or SPC.

SPC is one way by which quality control can be taken back from the inspection stage to the processes where work is done. Perhaps its best-known disciple today is Dr W. E. Deming, a former friend and colleague of Shewhart's. As Deming puts it, before you start to apply statistics, a process is likely to be in unstable chaos. Statistical control then opens the way for engineering innovation. So statistics introduce order where previously there was disorder, and the way is paved for still more quality gains. Furthermore, by introducing objective rather than subjective terms for quality within the context of the process, communication on quality issues between management and the operatives becomes possible. SPC does not inevitably lead to quality. Instead, it is a tool with which process quality can be achieved.

What is SPC?

SPC involves the application of the Shewhart control chart, or its principle, together with at least the rudiments of statistical methods needed to support it, such as statistical sampling, the use of graphs, histograms and check-sheets. Samples of data on the critical characteristics of the product are then randomly selected and their average and range values calculated. Sample-size is usually 5–12. These values are then plotted on separate charts, on which target values have been set so that the deviation of the outcomes from specifications will be apparent. Control limits are established from the samples' standard deviation. Upper and lower warning and action limits are then set, usually 1.98 and 3.09 times the standard deviation above the target value, and similarly below, though sometimes these figures are abbreviated to two and three times. The process can be considered to be statistically controlled if samples fall inside the warning limits, or with, at most, a statistically insignificant number falling outside.

When a process is in statistical control, the probability can be stated that observed data will fall within the given limits. The output from that process may still be variable, but the causes of any such variability are inherent in the process itself. Shewhart calls them 'chance causes'.

Where observations fall outside the warning limits this is because other factors have come into play: the causes of variation do not belong to a controlled system. These he calls 'assignable causes'. Assignable causes have been registered by the control chart and the opening phase of quality improvement is to isolate them, determine their origin and rectify matters. Defective incoming material may be a prominent source, operator error another. Assignable causes should be eliminated and whether this is done progressively or at a single stroke, as with a 'right first time' directive, will depend largely on the circumstances.

Once in statistical control, the chance causes of a system may be worked upon. This is typically a much longer job which can proceed only by increments. Clearly, the control chart warning limits can influence the accepted specification: if it is too fine there will inevitably be much rejected product. Essentially, however, the two concepts are quite separate. If a process is currently incapable of delivering a product efficiently there is no alternative but to improve it as rapidly as possible.

Although others independently developed aspects of SPC, Shewhart's is the name most frequently quoted, partly for his invention of the control chart in 1924 but perhaps above all for his demonstration of the scope and capabilities of applied statistical methods. The range and detail of the examples in his major work, *Economic Control of Quality of Manufactured Product* (1931), is such that readers at the time could immediately have started to apply SPC as widely as the Japanese were to do 20 years later. The really surprising feature of SPC is how little the subject has changed over the intervening years. There have been some refinements and developments to control charts, but essentially the subject is the same. Certainly, it was open to anyone to apply the technique after the appearance of Shewhart's book.

Why did the West not exploit its lead?

SPC was immediately recognised and acclaimed in statistical circles in the early 1930s, but organisations were slow to apply it. A large SPC training programme was organised by a US government agency in the early 1940s to raise quality in the war effort and in 1945 the UK Ministry of Supply started to do something similar. However, neither programme continued for long after the end of the hostilities. The initiative was generally not sustained by those who had benefited and the technique fell into disuse until taken up by the Japanese.

The paradox of SPC is that, if it is such an attractive and valuable technique, why was it not used widely and effectively from the outset? Why did the English-speaking world lose the advantage of a head-start? How can it be that, to this day, there are exhortations to use more SPC and hire more statisticians while researchers still report hostility in certain UK sectors and only localised use among smaller firms? Even where SPC *is* applied it seems largely to have been adopted in response to pressure from a specific customer or to comply with a quality-assurance standard. There are few cases of companies that have independently identified SPC as a necessary technique and then implemented it. Why should this be?

Whatever the reasons for the slow acceptance of SPC, it is not the lack of literature on the subject. Shewhart's book might be considered a lengthy work, the understanding of which requires a grounding in statistics, but shorter and more accessible treatments soon appeared in several countries. Among them is E. S. Pearson's masterly *The Application of Statistical Methods to Industrial Standardisation and Quality Control* (1935), written after Shewhart had visited London in 1932 and published by the British Standards Institution. Subsequently, BSI has played a leading role in the dissemination of SPC; it has published numerous standards down the years to introduce, explain and apply statistical methods to quality problems.

Numerous other books have appeared, several of them primarily addressed to quality. Many of their authors started as statisticians and only later became associated with industrial questions, so that statistics are given pride of place. As a result, some people complain elsewhere that statistics are being over-sold!

Mixed terminology

A minor irritation in the SPC literature is the profusion of terminology. This is not a source of difficulty for statisticians but can be for others. 'Statistically controlled' may be found also as 'statistically uniform', 'assignable causes' as 'special causes', 'chance causes' as 'random causes' or more frequently as 'common causes'. It is hard to see why anyone departed from Shewhart's terms.

Personnel difficulties

Part of the difficulty concerned with implementing SPC has been a shortage of expertise combined with organisational hurdles, so precluding the best use of what was available. In the days when SPC had to be put in at a relatively low level in an organisation, the information, skills and experience needed for such an introduction were beyond the capabilities and educational standards of the workers of the time. Managers were reluctant to become involved in what was seen as a low-grade technique, and statisticians were in short supply. It would have been difficult to hire anyone with the necessary training and ability. Even if taken on, such a person would have been unlikely to be satisfied with a lowly position for long. One frequent recommendation is that more people should be trained in statistics and somehow integrated with industry.

However, there are other problems for which this is not the remedy. Some of the limitations of SPC are indicated by the experience of those who have taken it on as an isolated measure. Quality improvements were difficult to find, and partly as a result, the initiative was hard to sustain. Even the Japanese had disappointing results with SPC during the first few years. Today we know that if SPC is to be accepted and used then our corporate culture and our attitudes towards quality must be changed. Above all, if changes have to be made so that quantitative techniques can be used at all, whether for quality or for any other purpose, there is likely to be a managerial problem. So, instead of SPC being one of the first measures taken, it should be part of a wider programme in which it is one of the last things to be done.

Criticism of manually operated SPC

Statisticians have made great promises for SPC, but these have proved difficult to achieve in the UK. SPC took control of quality away from inspection, focusing instead on the processes where error could occur; however, when it was operated with an entirely manual approach, there arose problems comparable to some of the shortcomings of an inspection function. For example, picture an industrial process with unacceptable and statistically unpredictable characteristics, and consequently with disruption, low productivity and variation in the output specification. Clearly, here is a prime case for the application of SPC. Management therefore implements SPC, with control charts and extensive participation from the process operatives, assignable causes are eliminated, the control limits are gradually reduced and the output approaches target specification more and more closely. An unqualified success for SPC? Not necessarily. As the operatives faithfully collect and plot data, the stage will eventually be reached where perfection is close. Now the plots will show minimal variation – preferably none at all. Thus *absolute* perfection is unlikely to be reached using this method alone, as monotony sets in and the charting exercise is seen as superfluous and redundant.

The traditional manual approach to SPC requires a stream of errors and corrective feedback to maintain the operators' attention. Indeed, for this reason alone it is doubtful in many situations whether anything more than the outstanding assignable causes can be overcome. Besides, interest is inevitably harder to sustain when working on 'chance' causes. The improvements are likely to be smaller, harder to make and phased over a longer time period. Some of them, too, will bear little or no relation to the operators' work experience. What is needed here is a simple system of automation for the data collection and management; this might need to do nothing more than indicate when a sample is outside the control limits (say, once every million cycles).

Today's electronic technology makes it possible to sustain the application of SPC and achieve a degree of conformance to specification, which was almost certainly beyond the ability of even the most dedicated process operator in Shewhart's day. Furthermore, the introduction of automation is likely to change the status of the participants. Although operators will still need to be involved, the huge job of working control charts manually may not be, and this could preclude some of the reasons for taking quality issues back to the workforce. Matters such as exactly what everyone does, who has responsibility and authority for a process and what the information flows should be will deserve close attention in each situation.

SPC in service activities

The principles of SPC may be applied readily to service industries, where appropriate data can be easily derived but that is the limitation. Most treatments of SPC mention services but invariably discuss the subject in terms of manufacturing industry. Manufacturing involves discrete, tangible products which may be assessed and measured: specifications are set in numerical terms and are open to precise appraisal. This can be the case with services, too, but frequently the collection of data is difficult, time-consuming and expensive – so much so that it becomes harder to discern the applications for SPC. Raise the cost of an SPC exercise and the benefits of the scheme become ever more difficult to justify.

Gains from SPC

Many strong cases for the use of SPC are to be found in the literature on quality and their message is that, if SPC is applied, quality will be developed. In reality it is not quite so simple: there are personnel problems, training issues, organisational difficulties, inaccuracy from manual methods and more. Even those organisations which persevere are rewarded with just a series of small, widespread incremental gains yet if this is the only benefit, it is hard for an organisation to get inspired about the prospect. A glance at history is even more discouraging. Organisations have tried SPC with indifferent results and, for understandable reasons, thereafter neglected it. Nations tried it during the war, yet ignored it later. Even the Japanese had to persevere with little reward for several years during the early 1950s before reaching success.

Much of the disappointment with SPC seems to have arisen from the expectation that quality would spring from the elimination of assignable causes and a reduction of chance causes, when perhaps the greater gain comes from the use of statistically controlled processes. If SPC is used on its own these gains will be wasted and an exercise generating only a few of the potential benefits is obviously harder to justify. Improvements from controlled processes depend on the amount done with them, and the possible gains are not just to specification conformance but also to the productivity of capital and labour.

The group of techniques through which SPC is integrated into operations and logistics management is known in Japan as Just in Time, or JIT.

Process quality without SPC

Before we examine JIT, we should look at two methods by which product quality can be achieved without the use of SPC.

The first of these is known as 'fool-proofing' or 'fail-safing'. This involves making some process or design change so that variation cannot be introduced to the product. A number of simple methods have been isolated for this purpose; they are described in S. Shingo's book *Zero Quality Control* (1986). Nearly all fool-proofing techniques make only a limited contribution to product quality and some are really just applied common sense. But, used in combination in the right set of circumstances, the techniques can create a process in which SPC becomes irrelevant to product quality. Any gains from SPC in a fool-proofed situation have therefore to come from statistically controlled processes alone. Normally, though, fool-proofing is intended merely to make a contribution to product quality, however valuable that contribution might be.

The second way to avoid using SPC in the field of product quality is to make a design 'robust' in relation to production and operator performances. This concept is similar to some methods of fool-proofing, but the approach is very different. Those critical

14

performance parameters that are potentially open to variation are isolated and interference with them is simulated, in part by the use of statistical methods. In the light of the results, designs are modified so that they can withstand any feasible sources of variation. Once again, this does not mean that SPC has been eliminated, since there are other reasons for having processes in statistical control.

The design of 'robust' products is most widely associated today with the name of Genichi Taguchi, who has been foremost in promoting not only the concept but also some of the statistical techniques by which it may be approached. However, the idea is not new, and some of Taguchi's statistical methods have been criticised as defective, inefficient and unnecessarily complicated by, among others, G. E. P. Box and B. Gunter.

JUST IN TIME

J IT takes its name from the practice, developed in Japan, of delivering goods frequently and in relatively small quantities to a production process which holds minimal inventory or none at all. To make such a system work, the incoming goods evidently have to be delivered 'just in time'. The technique appeared first in the late 1950s in Japanese shipyards to schedule deliveries of steel, as ships' plates create a substantial inventory problem. As most of the Japanese yards are, in all but name, vertically integrated with nearby steel mills, it was relatively simple to synchronise production plans: inventories were reduced and the new procedure created facilities which could respond more rapidly to market demand. Since the tempo of shipbuilding has always fluctuated widely, the consequent flexibility of output proved to be an important competitive factor.

The concept of JIT spread to Toyota, the company which has done the most to develop it. Here was an altogether more complicated situation than the shipyards, with more complex operations, greater variety of output and, above all, many more suppliers. A series of incremental improvements were introduced, and the subsequent process of change has never ended. Opening inventories were reduced and the number of suppliers fell; those who remained were en-couraged to create an appropriate defect-free stream of incoming

15

components. To take advantage of these developments it was then necessary to smooth the flow of work through Toyota's processes. This reduced the cost of work in progress and made the facilities more responsive to a change in production tempo. Batch sizes could therefore be reduced so that Toyota could respond more closely to the desires of the final customer. Gradually 'JIT' has come to be used as a collective term for a range of techniques that improve, speed and smooth the flow of operations from suppliers through to the market, while allowing much greater product variety to be handled.

A recent report by C. Voss and D. Clutterbuck has identified around 100 techniques covered by JIT. These are classified into

- manufacturing techniques
- production materials control
- JIT purchasing
- organisation for change

Many of the techniques, such as workforce flexibility, rapid equipment set-up, preventive maintenance and inventory control, may be used independently (and have been for years) without any reference to quality. Some are not in themselves quantitative methods but even these work better in combination and confer incremental quality improvements. For some of them, the fact that the relevant processes are in a state of statistical control might not be strictly necessary, but all will work better if this is the case. In the end, the producer is able to compete with rapid delivery at an appropriate price, and so conform more closely to what the customer wants.

Kanban system

One of the most widely known JIT techniques, though little used in the UK, is the Japanese Kanban system of manufacturing control. A Kanban is a work-station signboard holding a set of cards which are moved between locations. An incoming card is a signal to release a certain batch of product to the work-station downstream, while other cards are sent for supplies from upstream as these are needed. Basic information on the cards is what to produce, when and in what quantity, where it is to go and how. The Kanban system is thus an automatic directional device for work in progress.

To a Western observer, some features of this system might seem as obsolete as the punch cards formerly used in computer peripherals (although maybe the Japanese have already automated it without telling anyone). Furthermore the number of cards, or signals in use, must be kept as small as possible, with flows which are simple and direct. It is certainly possible to work the Kanban system in a complicated plant: Toyota use it in their car-manufacturing facilities. Nevertheless, anyone else about to try it might question whether, without extensive practice and development, the system is applicable to anything more than a simple sub-assembly.

Disregarding the mechanics of the system for a moment, its principle deserves the closest attention as it is organised to respond directly to market pressures. Incoming orders are first sorted and then scheduled to create as even a pace of activity as possible at the work-station during the prospective time period, typically a day. The work-stations furthest downstream then trigger the production flow against the sorted incoming orders and progressively activate stations upstream as their minimal work in progress is exhausted. Eventually, external suppliers are contacted through a re-order system. Such an upward flow of information for supplies can be compared directly with the traditional pattern, whereby a production plan is produced centrally in response to incoming orders. The plan is distributed to work-stations that are not necessarily in direct contact with each other and re-ordering is based on the anticipated production schedule rather than the actual output. Working inventories thus need to be higher, the production cycle is slower and the flow of operations is more likely to have discontinuities than if the proceedings are related directly to demand.

Objections to introducing JIT

JIT is presented as a set of technical measures, as this is how it is perceived in Japan, but applications in other countries may not be quite so simple. For example, the current pattern of suppliers might be only partly determined by operational factors and certain issues might need to be considered before any change is introduced. JIT completely fails to address problems such as this. The relative bargaining power of supplier and purchaser could be one factor, while innovation and product development might be another. Security of supply has often been a major concern in the UK and though JIT may offer benefits which outweigh such considerations, the choice is unlikely to be a straightforward one.

Similarly, the application of JIT methods among operations may not be quite as easy as the Japanese example suggests. A precondition for most JIT techniques is the prior use of SPC, to get operations into statistical control. This may be taken for granted in Japan, but not in the UK.

Another operational limitation is introduced by personnel questions. Most JIT applications require, if not the enthusiasm, then at least the active cooperation of the workforce, while opposition and demarcation problems will stop the introduction of the new method altogether. Some of the problems of implementing JIT may be compared with the record of the plant-optimisation studies of a generation ago. Quantitative methods first indicated that very large production units gave the potential for lower costs, and then helped to design them, treating people as small cogs in the system. But in reality success depended not on aiming at a notional cost target but rather on achieving good industrial relations so that the facilities could actually be put to work. And so it is with JIT and SPC: if they are to be introduced successfully, organisations must tackle certain personnel issues and develop a strategic framework for quality.

3

Quality through workforce participation: zero defects and quality circles

ZERO DEFECTS

I f the generation of product quality has be taken back from the inspection stage to the processes, and if the quality techniques work only if there are appropriately trained and motivated people, does it not make sense to concentrate on the people and treat the techniques as incidentals? Techniques may be vitally important, of course, but correct attitudes are absolutely essential. Quality is about people: about motivation, participation, leadership and training. What is needed therefore is management by walking about, not the blind implementation of a prescribed set of techniques. Such an approach, widely recommended elsewhere, provides an appealing recipe which, in the right place, can offer the promise of inexpensive and rapid quality improvement. However, one snag, noted by W. E. Deming, is that if you are to manage by walking about, you must first know the right questions to ask. Besides, attitudes are partly contingent on a range of other features – techniques, the structure, training – and something can be lost if these are ignored. This has been a difficulty with some participatory programmes intended in part to stimulate attitudes. Some of their limitations may be illustrated by looking at the topics of zero defects and quality circles.

Zero-defects programmes, far better known in the USA than in the UK, have had a mixed history. The term has been used to cover two distinct concepts; it has been associated with some disappointments, with much misdirected effort and generally, it has been discredited. The shortcomings of pioneer zero-defects programmes may be a reason why they have not been more widespread in the UK, but the main cause for their neglect was probably managerial inertia and lack of concern for quality issues in the 1960s, when such programmes were more heavily promoted. However, they do have a positive side, while some of the pitfalls are easily avoided.

Zero defects for the Pershing missile

The first zero-defects programme arose in 1960 at Martin Marietta, a defence contractor producing a medium-range nuclear missile, the Pershing, for the US Army at Orlando, Florida. The programme was remarkably successful. The prototypes delivered had a number of defects, any one of which could impair the working and reliability of a missile in service. Elimination of these was just possible through a particularly elaborate inspection procedure, but such an approach would have been impracticable for the forthcoming production run, being prohibitively time-consuming and costly. However, the US Army required not only zero defects for delivered missiles but also an accelerated delivery schedule, for these were tense times in the Cold War. There had just been the crisis over the erection of the Berlin Wall and, although of course no one could have foreseen it at the time, the Cuban missiles crisis would erupt soon after production had started.

Traditional inspection-based methods could not deliver the necessary results – and certainly not on time – so it was clear from the outset that something new had to be tried. Attitudes and motivation appeared to be central to the problems at Martin Marietta. Both management and workforce had come to accept that mistakes were inevitable. An analysis showed that most defects arose at stages associated with operatives, and one conclusion drawn was that, if only the workforce could produce perfectly, the necessary standard could be reached. Accordingly, a campaign was promoted heavily throughout the company to instil into everyone the necessity and feasibility of producing defect-free missiles to an accelerated schedule. The aspect that received the most publicity was the process whereby individual employees were first persuaded that the target of zero defects was both necessary and possible and then that they should sign pledges promising that henceforth they would not produce faulty work. Minor incentives were given for this commitment, but the principal reward was personal recognition. The first defect-free production missile was delivered at the end of 1961.

The idea of zero defects spread to other corporations and apparently had some initial success. Gradually, however, it was noticed that quality was largely unaffected and that any contribution made by a zero-defects drive was likely to be very small. Part of the explanation for this was that, as with almost every managerial innovation, the new ideas were taken on first by the most progressive organisations; what the best can do with a fresh technique may be beyond the powers of the less able to emulate, even though in the latter case there is clearly greater scope for improvement. Programmes tended to be launched in a carnival-style fashion, with as many employees as possible persuaded to commit to defect-free working; thus, rather than focusing on quality, such drives became more akin to employee-motivational techniques, combining management by objectives with a steak lunch. It was all relatively inexpensive and harmless enough in itself, but it did not do what it was supposed to do: raise quality. Its real cost came about through the poor quality delivered before the shortcoming was recognised and another approach tried.

Who controls the processes?

Much of the effectiveness of these zero-defects programmes hinged on who could alter the output of a process. Some research in the early 1960s had shown that around 85 per cent of all defects were associated with operator error. It was therefore concluded that only appropriate attitudes and improved standards of workmanship on the shop floor could raise quality, as with the experience at Martin Marietta. However, some previous research, dating from the early 1950s and reported by J. M. Juran and F. A. Gryna (see Bibliography) attributed the same proportion of defects – 85 per cent – to processes and systems over which management had control. The workforce might have been associated with the processes but, without authority, could not be responsible for change. Juran and Gryna concluded that quality improvement is predominantly an issue for management and that attempts to delegate it, through a zero-defects programme or otherwise, are misplaced and destined to achieve, at best, limited results.

Experience with zero-defects programmes in the USA suggests that of these two interpretations Juran's view was closer to reality. Certainly, the question of who *should* have responsibility and authority for quality and who actually *has* it deserves close attention. But whether 85 per cent of processes can be taken as falling under management control is open to doubt: the figure, although still widely quoted, relies on work done long ago. Without details of the relevant processes, conditions, training of operatives, the organisational structures and so on, it is not clear how closely it matches today's circumstances. There are grounds for believing that the allocation of operational authority varies widely.

The Pershing project re-examined

If the delegation of responsibility is inappropriate because the vast majority of systems are outside the control of the operatives concerned, it may be questioned why the original zero-defects programme at Martin Marietta worked so well. Zero-defects pledges may have played a part but there were also other factors in operation. Moreover, it is possible that elsewhere the attention given to those features affecting the workforce led to others being neglected.

The Pershing project had several distinguishing features: none were unique, but the combination of all of them was unusual. One report gave the Pershing prototypes a defect rate of about one component in 1,000; another gave it one in 2,000. The precise figure makes little difference to the argument here: on either ratio, the finished product compared very favourably with norms in other manufacturing sectors of the time. Furthermore, although we do not have full details of the nature of the defects, it seems they were overt and sufficient to impair operational performance. Although serious in themselves and quite unacceptable to the customer, they were much easier to put right than, for example, defects created by the narrowing of statistically defined acceptance limits across a wide range of components. Thus, from the standpoint of defects alone, there was little wrong with the Pershing at the start of the exercise.

Aside from Martin Marietta's production performance, most aspects of the Pershing's quality were high – indeed, very high. Design and specification had reached an advanced stage. The customer's requirements were met so well that accelerated delivery was demanded, something which surely can be regarded as the ultimate accolade for a marketing effort! Few situations can enjoy such a simple and clear-cut focus for a quality drive. Fewer still are likely to share such a readily apparent sense of purpose with which all could identify; in the USA of the early 1960s the production of nuclear missiles had many of the attributes of a noble cause.

Compare this with the scenario facing some of the zero-defects programmes which followed. Questions of design and specification may have been covered, but the programmes did not address them. Whether the prospective customers needs were to be met well or just adequately was unknown – often the programme participants were not even alerted to the issue. The nature of the defects which they were intended to put right might also be unknown, and sometimes were difficult both to define and to identify. Frequently, too, severe defects do not jeopardise the viability of the final product but merely degrade performance and gradually lower the subjective perception of overall quality. The gains from less rework, fewer returns, lower inventories, faster set-up times and all the rest may mean a lot to higher management but very little to the operatives. Somehow it is easier to inspire an organisation when its objective can be couched in terms of national defence.

Another singular aspect of the zero-defects scheme at Martin Marietta was the calibre of some of the people associated with it. One of the executives, J. F. Halpin, wrote up the project in a book, *Zero Defects*, published in 1966. Two others who left a few years later to join ITT wrote books on quality, J. T. Hagen becoming well known in the subject and P. B. Crosby becoming very well known. Perhaps the environment at Martin Marietta was conducive to the development of such paragons; perhaps the presence of such flair was a factor in the success of the zero-defects programme – who knows? Get the people right in an organisation and things can happen which otherwise might be impossible.

Zero defects as a management standard

Despite the later disappointments with zero-defects programmes, the concept lives on: articles are written and conferences arranged. The implication is that, if everyone would only work more carefully, quality would emerge. However, a much more convincing argument for zero defects is advanced by P. B. Crosby. He maintains that the mistake was to aim zero-defects schemes (and even then only their practical features) at lower-ranking employees. Rather than being a performance goal for the shop floor, zero defects should be seen as a management standard. The concept cannot easily be misunderstood or misinterpreted: it says that only the best will do and such an absolute standard is essential for management.

Support for zero defects as a management standard has come from Japan, where the system has been widely used since 1964, and from J.M. Juran and F.M. Gryna who, in discussing the quality improvements organisations should be aiming for, introduce two new concepts, *control* and *breakthrough*. Control is a state of significant but limited improvement; it aims essentially at doing things as well as possible within the limits of the *status quo*, and may be approached incrementally. Breakthrough, on the other hand, represents an improvement to unprecedented levels of quality. It is a great leap forward achieved not by doing better what has been done in the past but by taking a completely fresh approach. Most of the objections to any prospective drive towards breakthrough come from middle management, for whom zero defects is seen as a more realisable objective.

A final reflection on conditions at Martin Marietta is that, if opposition to change is likely to come primarily from middle management, the accelerated delivery of Pershings required by the US Army may have been an important factor in the success of the programme. Virtually any change has its detractors. If it takes place slowly, there is time to arrange obstruction – but introduce a deadline and obstructive, bureaucratic processes have less chance of being brought into play. Whether wittingly or not, the US Army helped to overcome what has proved to be the prime stumbling block for other quality programmes.

Zero defects at Martin Marietta achieved much. The programme was put together with imagination and executed with flair. It is not necessarily to be copied exactly, because its conditions were unusual, but many of its lessons are important and some of the mistakes made later are particularly instructive when considering quality circles.

QUALITY CIRCLES

Quality circles are a comparatively recent feature of organisational life. The first was started as late as 1962 in Japan, where they spread at an astonishing speed, their numbers reaching five figures by 1970. They enjoyed their most rapid phase of growth in the next decade, passing into six figures by 1980. Coinciding as it did with the increasing recognition of improved Japanese manufacturing quality in the West, this expansion may help to explain why the practice became identified as the prime Japanese quality method. After all, Japan was a country whose quality had, within living memory, been very low indeed. Here, too, was the technique of the moment, spreading at an astounding pace. Surely the system must be the key to quality generation, so why not use it as a quick fix for the West's quality problems? The lessons of history warned that such an approach might prove not to be so simple, but they were largely ignored.

Quality circles in Japan: background and nature

In the drive for better quality in Japanese industry, quality circles were a late development. A strong commitment to improving quality had been widely accepted in the late 1940s among Japanese senior management: BS600 on statistical process control had been translated into Japanese in 1941; US occupation forces in 1946 had introduced the SPC programme used for US wartime production; and a closer investigation of the methods used at the Bell Telephone Laboratory had led to an invitation to Dr W. E. Deming to visit Japan a couple of years afterwards. The implementation of quality programmes, based on SPC, started widely from 1950. This was some 12 years before the appearance of the first quality circle.

The initial results from this 1950 initiative were limited and disappointing. It appears this was for much the same reasons that quality programmes in other countries likewise failed. SPC was aimed at raising quality through the detail of processes only, yet if those processes were to be controlled by management, then management issues, problems and shortcomings would have to be the first to be addressed if quality was to be improved.

A broader view of the nature of quality was established in Japan after a 1954 lecture tour by J. M. Juran, and the pace of improvement accelerated. This did not imply that SPC was irrelevant – on the contrary, it can make an essential contribution to many processes at appropriate stages of a quality programme – but the detail involved can be substantial and the people frequently in the best position to handle it are those closest to the processes, namely the shop-floor workers. Thus the quality circle emerged as a structure whereby part of the responsibility for better process control could be delegated and higher conformance to specification attained. It was a major step in the promotion of SPC for the Japanese.

In Japan quality circles are generally composed of groups of workers from the same production process or production area who have come together in the attempt to improve quality. Membership, although subject to some organisational pressures, is intended to be voluntary and in reality is likely to be substantially so. Circles meet in a combination of lunchbreaks, paid time and (significantly) in unpaid time after hours. The principal methods used are simple and practical techniques, putting SPC into effect, making better use of it and widening the understanding of its results. Training covers SPC, the gathering, organising and interpreting of statistics, and education in some problem-solving techniques. The circle is therefore given a grounding in SPC, in histograms, scatter diagrams with graphs, Pareto analysis, cause-and-effect diagrams, brainstorming and so on. Rewards and recognition for the circles' results are given collectively. They are shared among the members, and regarded as highly important.

The impetus to form quality circles in Japan appears to come mostly if not entirely from management. Managers act as facilitators for the emerging circles, are available to give advice and information and, critically, provide the subsequent channels through which results are communicated. Thus Japanese quality circles are strongly institutionalised and to Western eyes it may seem amazing they ever got started. Such voluntary groupings, enjoying so much influence, managerial support, active encouragement and open communications, would from the outset require the effective working of a certain style of enlightened organisation that is not often seen in the West.

Japanese organisational charts are characterised by several hierarchy tiers, with promotion and seniority partly dependent on age. In a Western organisation such a structure might be expected to lead to obstruction, opposition and poor communications from the lower ranks upwards, but in Japan the corporate culture transforms such conditions. Although nominal differences of rank, status and function exist theoretically, the reality is decidedly less formal than in other countries. Contacts and communications around the organisation are better and participation of the workforce in decisions is typically an established practice. Against such a background, quality circles might be seen as a technique for whose success these unique Japanese circumstances could be crucial.

But there is a question about what most of the quality circles in Japan actually achieve. Any number of examples of substantial contributions can be quoted, but there is doubt as to just what can be expected from a randomly selected circle in a large plant in provincial Japan. Indeed, it seems that most do not instigate major quality developments but are justified instead by a combination of employee motivation and a series of minor, incremental improvements to costs, productivity and general conformance to specifications. Thus circles have a plant-orientated and product-orientated outlook, and most of their purpose has been to put SPC into effect. Sometimes this is neither all that is needed for process quality nor the most suitable approach. One criticism, expressed even in Japan, is that many process problems need to be solved on the spot or, preferably, before they occur, whereas circles can only start to discuss shortcomings after they have happened. The use of circles can also have the disadvantage of encouraging people to identify far too strongly with their group, whereas total quality really needs identification with the aims and objectives of the organisation as a whole.

More generally, there is also the censure that, to an even greater extent than with SPC itself, quality circles relate only to manufacturing industry. Circles can be set up in service activities, but they require several workers operating close to each other and on the same or very similar tasks. Such conditions are less easily found in the services than in manufacturing, especially as the trend today is towards still fewer departments where numerous personnel are engaged on routine activities.

Quality circles elsewhere: some problems

The first quality circle in the USA was started at Lockheed in 1974, and the idea spread to the UK a few years later. Initial reports were encouraging. This attitude was coloured by the fact that those who were early in the field tended already to have a strong awareness and enthusiasm for quality, while some cases had a reputation for quality that was already extremely high. But soon, as circles were adopted more widely, the picture changed. Either they were very hard to keep going or else, usually after 18 months, they broke up. Whatever their effects on motivation, the influence on quality was in many instances low or negligible.

What had gone wrong? A procedure developed for Japanese conditions was inappropriate for a direct transplant elsewhere. Most of the difficulties may have been easy to isolate, but some were very hard to rectify. Simple points, such as the identification of the workforce with the aims and objectives of the organisation are time-consuming to change, yet the Japanese had enjoyed a head start. Industrial-relations patterns, too, had to be handled very carefully and new procedures adjusted accordingly. Thus circle operation on the exact Japanese pattern proved to be extremely rare, with very few people operating out of hours or in unpaid time.

Another problem was the commitment from senior management in the UK. This could be detected from insufficient training compared with Japan, where educational levels, particularly in mathematics, are higher among shop-floor operatives. But above all, perhaps, were the failings of middle management. Rather than handle the job directly, quality-circle facilitators were appointed with responsibility for establishing procedures but without sufficient authority to do so. Communications – both down to and away from – the circles were poor so long as managers ignored them. Not surprisingly, it is now possible to find the view that quality circles are just another cynical employee-motivation programme in which management delegates quality issues as a way of getting rid of them.

Getting quality circles to work

A survey carried out on UK quality circles for the Manpower Services Commission by B. G. Dale and J. Lees in 1986 found that, while the original pattern of Japanese circles should not be forgotten, any practical measures needed to be adapted towards a particular situation and its culture. Enthusiasm for the concept remained strong despite previous disappointments, and some general principles seemed to raise the chances of success. Circles work best, for instance, when part of an overall quality management system which is evidently supported from the top: thus the chief executive should establish attitudes that encourage quality and ensure that communications are open; he or she needs also the support and commitment of all managers and, if some of them are actively involved in the new development, so much the better. Support from trade-union representatives evidently raises the likelihood of establishing successful circles, as too does their association with enthusiastic and committed facilitators.

The establishment of a quality circle should not represent too large a step in the implementation of quality measures. Difficulties can arise here with SPC, which is not very widely used among medium-sized companies in the UK. Clearly, some preparation will be needed to avoid introducing quality circles and SPC simultaneously. Moreover, training will have a major role in reducing the impact of new measures. At its best, training can be inspiring as well as informative, and thereby become a motivational factor. It should be very much an on-going process, so that it sustains the enthusiasm critical to nearly all quality circles.

Although a simple step in itself, the forming of quality circles implies a measure of cultural change. It requires the greater involvement in a corporate activity of people who often have had no previous influence or responsibility at all and may even be antagonistic to the organisation and the authority of its management. Almost certainly there will be more delegation than in the past, as certain decisions become decentralised to groups of employees whose trust must be won. Loyalty must be built up so that, in return, higher productivity and better quality can be achieved. In short, it is a two-way process. Such matters can take a long time before they result in an improved organisational performance.

The success of quality circles depends also on both the nature of the process on which a group is concentrating and its relationship to what goes before and what follows. Some situations have much greater scope for improvement than others. Statistics and other information may be readily available, while errors can be easily identified and corrected by the operatives themselves. Where management has to be involved, clear recommendations can readily be made by the members of the quality circle. Complicate any of these processes, however, and a circle's output is limited, no matter how capable and enthusiastic the members are.

Quality circles and total-quality management

Within the perspective of a total-quality programme, quality circles cover only a single part of the areas in which improvements can be made and in most organisations this part is likely to be a minor one. Poor marketing, defective designs and specifications, unwise pricing, irregularities in the quality and delivery of supplies and in the activities both upstream and downstream – all of these will be almost entirely outside the scope of the circles' deliberations. It may be possible for a circle to influence some of those responsible for such matters, but certainly it will be an outstanding circle that manages to effect this in a large organisation.

However, circles can perceive poor quality elsewhere even if they cannot act directly to improve it and poor quality is demotivating from the top to bottom of the organisation. Thus improvement in one area has an effect on constructive developments elsewhere. Piecemeal efforts may be quite out of place for comprehensive measures can demonstrate results whose scale is not apparent from a series of small steps. Get a total-quality programme started and a point can come where quality circles are an easy, inexpensive and worthwhile step. Implementation involves appointing circle facilitators, preferably from the ranks of the existing managers, and then it is their task to start the training.

4

Quality through design

WHAT IS DESIGN?

The public's awareness of design has risen so much in the last generation that virtually everyone must have a view of what design actually is. Literally dozens of definitions may be found, with varying emphasis on products and markets. The term 'design' is also used in terms of any of several activities and disciplines within an organisation. So it is possible to take a restrictive definition, yet for the purposes of quality, a broad view is needed.

Design covers the conception of a product or service to meet a perceived market need. The product's outline, its specification, what it does and how it works are design issues. It can be designed so that the effects of process variation are minimised, so that its conformance to specification is more likely to be close. It can also be designed so that it conforms to its specification long after purchase – in other words, to be reliable. Not surprisingly, on such a broad view, design is sometimes seen by the public as quality, and certainly it forms a major part of it. Significantly, design is done *before* production. SPC took quality control a stage back from inspection; a focus on design has taken it still further back.

In the past, design was held out as a competitive force which would increasingly benefit the UK's trading strength and it has been the subject of several government initiatives. Aspects of the UK's design strengths appear second to none, insofar as they can be compared directly with those of other countries. This widespread impression that available design skills are outstanding has meant that some of the shortcomings have seemed all the more disappointing. Somehow, the various features of design and production have not been integrated successfully into what the market wants quite as effectively as some of our international competitors. There have always been examples of UK organisations whose design would stand comparison with the best in the world, but they have been too few; the strength in depth was lacking. Most of the shortfall may be related to the management of design for quality.

Artistic or industrial design

There are at least three conceptions of design and the management of design is to combine appropriate elements of all three.

The first and possibly most widespread perception of design concerns aesthetic matters. The outline of an item, its shape, 'styling', colour and other details of its finish are all part of the design and the 'industrial designer' who decides them is usually seen as someone whose training is likely to have been outside the commercial and technical disciplines. Indeed, she or he is likely to be regarded as akin to an architect who happens to be turning a hand to products rather than buildings.

A product's function and performance might be influenced by artistic questions, but for the most part they are seen as issues for an engineer. Just where this second design element, engineering, starts and aestheticism stops is a moot point, but there are clearly situations in which one discipline dominates to the extent that the other makes no contribution whatsoever. Clearly, too, the balance of engineering design and industrial design varies – and should vary – widely between products.

Yet there is more to design than these two disciplines. Design has to take account of the needs of a market and the price it will bear. Such a decision will inevitably depend upon many production issues. There will thus be a contribution from several areas of management, principally marketing, but also including pricing, operations, finance, personnel and more. All of these contributions will affect the detail of what is actually produced, in however minor a way – and, on occasion, in some major ways. The London Business School's Design Management Unit calls this process 'silent design'. Most of the participants in the unit have not been trained formally in design, may be quite unaware they are contributing, and may even disagree that they have made a design contribution! But it is possible for 'silent design' to be the major influence on the design process, as for instance where a design is determined by a flow of market information and the method of its collection, processing and interpretation.

Design is a multi-disciplinary activity and the manager has to combine the relevant skills, encourage communications between the exponents of each of them and generate a sense of common purpose. The differences which have arisen over this in the past have been principally due to the split between industrial designers and engineers. Methods are different and backgrounds and affiliations are quite distinct and separate. Corporate cultures become conditioned and all of this can interfere with the design emphasis placed on a product. In the end, the design mix may be neither market-orientated nor even product-orientated but instead determined by the design view of the organisation and the way in which that view has been shaped by traditions and personalities.

Part of the blame for this state of affairs in the UK may be attributed to the educational system. Engineers are trained in engineering and technology while industrial designers read architecture or come from art schools. Quite apart from the differences in disciplines, there is the physical separation of the departments. The government has recognised this problem and attempted to promote unity, but this appears to have had little effect in the seats of learning beyond administrative issues, so the cultural gulf continues.

The development of competitive products from the UK's resources and design skills may be a management problem, but it has to be said that the designers themselves are not the easiest of people to manage.

THREE APPROACHES TO MANAGING DESIGN

The first objective in managing design and quality is likely to be to get the product right, in a market-orientated sense. One approach is to manage intuitively, but few of us have the necessary genius to perceive in advance what the market will want at the time when it is possible to deliver. There are, though, some very important examples, particularly among new products, where only an inspired vision of the uses to which something would be put could have started to give an indication of the ultimate size of the market. Using elaborate methods might have clouded the vision which was essential in such cases to sustain the product's development.

A second approach, which may also be used where market information is incomplete or impossible to obtain, is to make a series of limited moves and assess the market's reactions to them. Widely used either alone, or as part of the overall marketing programme, this exercise by its very nature leads to the generation of many mistakes, but they are limited ones, and help to guide future product development. However, accommodating such a series of disappointments while waiting for success is the principal difficulty of managing this reactive approach.

The intuitive and reactive approaches may have an essential part to play but, because of their limitations, most marketing and much design are done through planning: information is collected, organised and analysed, and conclusions are derived from it. The exercise centres on customers and competitors, against a background of the organisation's capabilities. Ideally there would be no limit to the amount of information collected before decisions were made, but in practice there are the constraints of time, cost and the sheer scale of the task. A basic outline might be:

- who are the customers?
- where are they?
- what do they need and how can their preferences be developed?
- when will the goods be required?
- what factors define the market and its size?
- what are you attempting to appeal to them on?

- will you be competing in terms of price?
- is the market a limited one?
- what are the particular, distinguishing features of your product?

On these limited questions alone a large stream of information can be built up, organised and related to the design function. Similarly there are questions about the competitors:

- who are they?
- what do they produce?
- how closely are they competing and on what characteristics?
- how do their prices, returns and costs compare with your own?
- how do their design effort and product-development speed compare?
- who reacts to changing markets most quickly?

Once again, there will be much information to analyse and present before the scene can be set for the artistic and engineering design contributions.

DESIGNING QUALITY IN

Once the market orientation of a design has been established, some product-oriented measures may be used to design quality in. The Taguchi method of making the product 'robust' relative to the production process and to the customers' use has already been mentioned (see page 15). There may also be scope for designing the product for ease of production in a manner which, while leaving quality to the customer unaffected, allows lower production costs. Both matters are a task for the engineers.

DESIGN, QUALITY AND COSTS

Design factors can make a product's manufacture more expensive, and the case for a quality programme rests in large measure on whether or not the increased returns outweigh the higher costs. The view expressed in some UK government papers and in at least one

BSI standard is that in raising product quality, a point comes after which returns will decline.

The view of US observers such as Deming, Juran and Crosby is that higher quality leads to greater sales, so – quite apart from reduced rework, disruption and inventories – the higher volume will in itself lead to greater profit. All that is needed, therefore, is to isolate rapidly the first three-quarters of the cost figures; the returns will then be seen to be so much greater as to justify fully the quality programme. Reality depends partly on some market characteristics as well as, crucially, on unit costs declining with volume – a plausible assumption in manufacturing, although less likely in services.

As well as publicising experimental simulation for design, G. Taguchi has helped shed some light on the contentious subject of the costs of quality and the returns thereby generated. He divides the design function into three parts: systems design, parameter design and allowance design. Systems design provides the functional outline of a product; improvements to quality at this stage can be expected to lead both to substantial falls in costs and to greater returns. Parameter design is concerned with the specifications, largely a matter for engineering, but here, too, a greater design effort may be expected to lead to lower costs and higher returns. Allowance design defines the tolerances and the degree of 'finish' a product has and generally, the higher the quality, the greater the production cost. A higher standard of allowance design may lead to increased returns, but there is likely to be a limit somewhere. Those who see better quality as entailing higher costs and final prices may have a conception of design in which allowance design is prominent.

DESIGN AS A COMPETITIVE PRECONDITION

It may be questioned whether evaluating design solely in terms of costs and immediate returns will ever give an adequate estimation of its worth, for design and quality are preconditions for future competitiveness. The option is thus not whether an organisation wants to use a design to generate greater returns, but whether it wants to continue in that particular activity over the medium or long term. If a strategy of low costs is chosen, for example, the prices should be the lowest in the sector. If design has any contribution to make at all to this process, someone else will be using it and so the low cost strategy may be jeopardised. Similarly, if the strategy aims to exploit market niches or to compete through distinguished products, design will be essential if a competitive presence is to be maintained; the question of the returns comes afterwards. Without design, strategic aims are confined to those few products and market niches where it makes only a minor contribution. Design and quality, in short, broaden strategic choice and make it more likely that an organisation will be larger and enjoy greater returns.

EDUCATION FOR DESIGN

As design is of such importance to quality and commercial competitiveness, it is vital that design education should be promoted widely. Within any organisation, people at all levels should be at least introduced to what marketing and design entail and to the disciplines and functions involved, with a coverage in greater depth for those at higher levels. A measure of customer awareness should be generated and then related through design and the production process to what is produced.

Elsewhere, the teaching of design is spreading and, since the establishment in the UK of the National Curriculum from 1989, will extend back to the primary schools. A possible split between art and design, on the one hand, and design and technology, on the other, might appear at first to offer scope for starting the traditional schism between engineering and industrial design from the earliest educational age. However, current proposals should avert the danger. Examples requiring both artistic and engineering solutions have been assembled with evident care, so questions of the primacy of one discipline or the other are unlikely to arise. Inevitably, the proposed curriculum is mostly product-orientated, but one of its surprising features is just how far it has been possible to introduce the topics of customer awareness, consumer preference and market-orientation.

The likely effects of the curriculum are such as to give grounds for great optimism for UK commercial life in the future.

The design scene in the UK is encouraging. There may have been disappointments in the past and there may still be much under-developed potential, but the position is improving and could get even better. If we are looking for signs that the UK might in the future be recognised internationally as a high-quality producer, some of the most compelling arguments in favour of this view are related to design.

5

Quality through published standards

PUBLISHED STANDARDS

Organisations operate to a variety of rules, yardsticks and standards, most of which they set for themselves. These may influence, condition and even determine aspects of design and operations, and so contribute to the development of quality. Also among the range of standards are those produced externally; typically widely available, these are usually purchased.

The aim of published standards is the production of the best achievable limits of quality on the feature in question. However, as this is often just a minor part of an overall design or production cycle, most published standards individually make only a small, localised contribution to the quality of the final product as a whole. An aspect of standardisation might, for instance, add nothing in itself to reliability, product consistency, productivity, reject rates or some other attribute widely associated with quality. But, if used in combination with other standards on design, quality-control techniques and quality assurance, it is highly likely that it will help to orient the organisation towards total quality.

There are several sources of published standards. Some are large organisations issuing what amount to specifications for their own requirements. The dominant UK source is the British Standards Institution, or BSI, an autonomous body which, although it still has some public funding, gets most of its income from the sale of standards and related services. (In some countries, electrical standards are handled separately, usually for the historical reason that it was in this sector that standards first had to be applied.)

International standards are increasingly important and are produced by agreement between the major national standards institutions or equivalent representative bodies. They can be applied directly in the UK, but approval is necessary if aspects of UK legislation are to apply to them. International standards create an avenue for overseas influence on UK industry, but the flow of information is very much a two-way process since BSI is recognised internationally as one of the best developed of all issuing authorities.

A few standards were issued by the European Commission in its early days, but these were not a success. Consequently, activities became confined to endorsing standards which support certain EEC aims and to influencing national institutions to develop standards in support of EC directives. The national standards bodies formed two small central organisations in Brussels, CENELEC and CEN, to help promote cooperation with the EEC, CENELEC covering electrical standards and CEN handling all other sectors. Now, with the prospect of a closer market in 1992, there is rising demand for a definitive set of European standards.

The rationale for published standards

Standards are essential to provide some of the technical content of Government, to improve matters which are inadequately served by market forces, such as health, safety, reliability, maintainability, and the conservation of resources, while trade barriers which might otherwise exist are prevented. A minority of standards, notably those on health and safety, are backed by statute and thus conformance to them is mandatory. Adherence to many others is essential to any producer who wishes to maintain a competitive market presence. This might appear to place published standards in conflict with one of the primary principles of free-market competition: surely the market should be left to provide customers with a range of suitable goods and a free choice? But it is often possible to achieve a higher level of quality for the customer through the use of standards than would be the case through the market mechanism alone. Organisations may present highly inadequate information to customers, and frequently a degree of technical knowledge is necessary if the customer is to make an informed selection. Also, situations can arise in which a combination of market dynamics and the simple mechanics of production prevents the emergence of the standardised design the customers *want* and consequently, the higher production volumes and lower unit costs fail to materialise. A solution could be agreed by a grouping of producers, but that might leave them open to the charge of forming a cartel; by contrast, the legalistic forum provided by a recognised standards authority avoids anti-monopoly legislation.

This broad rationale means that a standards body operating entirely as a private enterprise could cover only part of the field. Some standards (nearly all those on health) are absolutely essential yet have a very limited circulation. They are just as time-consuming as any other, so ways have to be found to subsidise or to charge for them at a level which market forces on their own could not support.

Forming a standard

The process of creating a standard starts when someone identifies a suitable need and contacts a standard-making authority. Obviously, the need is most likely to be expressed initially by a company, a trade association or the public sector, but the stimulus could come from anyone else – including a private individual. The standards authority first establishes whether or not a potential standard is feasible, for there are a variety of limitations to the scope of standards, mostly concerning possible market restrictions. (A standard must not limit a design; it must not prevent an alternative way of getting to the final result a product is intended to fulfil and patented systems cannot be made into standards. Use of the standards authority as an agency for a monopolistic influence thus has to be avoided.) On a wider plane, suspicions are frequently expressed that standards authorities are instruments of discriminatory trade practice. This is denied; in any case, the rise in importance of international standards is cause for believing that the national authorities are impartial. Nonetheless, the matter is evidently destined to be the object of vigilance from many quarters.

Having checked the provisional feasibility, the standards authority identifies and contacts the interested parties to establish a working committee. This then proceeds to work towards an agreement; the standards authority sits on the sideline, helping to promote the process if needed but not contributing technically. All of this is time-consuming. The Ministry of Defence quotes a record time of three weeks to produce one historic standard, but normally nine months is considered extremely fast! More generally, three years are likely to expire from the time the idea is first thought of to the appearance of the completed standard. The time span can be much longer, nearly all of it being consumed by technical committees working towards a consensus. In this context the word 'consensus' need not mean unanimity; it may instead mean a majority without significant opposition – and even this may be elusive. There is always the possibility that, after lengthy proceedings, no agreement and hence no standard can be attained.

Reviewing standards

As well as acting as a facilitator in the initial production process, the standards authority has also to handle the changes which occur to historic standards. At BSI all standards are formally reviewed at least every five years (more frequently if there is some special cause). Publications are updated by a combination of revisions and amendments. Although the dividing line between the two can be a moot point, whenever an amendment is made, the issue date of the original standard is changed to conform with the date of the amendment.

Three criticisms of standards

Most of the criticisms of published standards concern the time they take or are expected to take to produce. Three years is a long time to wait; long enough, indeed, to limit the fields to which the new standards can be applied. In sectors where there is considerable innovation or where there is rapid development and change, the delay can render the subsequent standard of little practical value.

In cases where a standard is essential, yet the lifecycle of the product is measured in months, a solution can be to go through the procedure of generating but not actually finalising a standard. Instead, the minutes of the committee are issued at frequent intervals. Thus anti-trust considerations are satisfied and appropriate agreement can be reached. Another procedure employed to speed implementation is the use of a provisional standard. This is a document which all involved agree to use and to change if necessary. It may become a full standard if still in use after a certain period, but initially it is not subjected to such a rigorous acceptance procedure as a full standard would be.

A further objection to standards is that they are heavily weighted towards larger organisations. When interested parties are being identified, larger organisations clearly have a higher profile simply by virtue of their size. More importantly, they have the resources to allocate the considerable amount of executive time required if the deliberations are to reach a result – which, of course, they may not do. But, if the production of standards is a matter for large companies, their use favours the small company at least as much. A standard shows effectively that a product built to the correct specifications and incorporating certain design and marketing features will satisfy the market. The advantage of possessing that information becomes greater the smaller a firm is, since smaller organisations might never, on their own, have been able to afford to duplicate the work involved in establishing the standard.

The volume and complexity of the information users have to master and then keep abreast of present a problem. Currently, BSI has about 11,000 published standards, the volume of material associated with them is rising, and the development of the international standards scene implies that matters will get ever more complicated. Luckily information storage, handling and presentation technology are more than keeping pace, so the likelihood is that, even with the increasing extent and complexity of the data, there will be a substantial reduction in the skill, time and space required to accommodate the latest standards.

STANDARDS AND QUALITY

The use of standards is rising, as is the public perception of them and the quality they help to generate. BSI's introduction from 1979 of the quality assurance standards (the BS5750 series) has been principally responsible for this. The USA may have been the first country to introduce the military development of quality assurance to many civilian suppliers through a civilian project, the Apollo programme, in the 1960s, but the UK was the first, in 1979, to provide a system of quality assurance suitable for universal application in the civilian domain. The use of quality assurance standards is now more widespread in the UK than anywhere else, with a lead of several years in their application. Today, there are nearly 10,000 organisations certified to BS5750, about 5,500 of whom have been handled by the certification arm of BSI itself. (The total includes nearly all of the suppliers initially assessed by the Ministry of Defence.)

The acceptance of BS5750 was very heavily promoted by the National Quality Campaign of 1982. A government White Paper, Cmnd.8621, issued in July of that year, endorsed quality assurance for civilian use and required BS5750 for the nationalised industries and for public-sector procurement generally. The pace of certification rose, and the gradual but widespread improvement in UK quality may be dated from around that time. BS5750 was adopted by the International Standards Organisation, or ISO, as the ISO 9000 series in 1987 and also as the European standard, EN29000, the following year.

6

Military procurement and the development of quality assurance

INFLUENCES

Developments in quality policy and techniques have seen many influences and contributions in the past: statisticians, producers, government agencies, craft guilds, livery companies . . . All of these and more have had profound and important effects. Outstanding among them, however, have been the effects of military procurement; indeed, as D. G. Spickernell noted, in the evolution of quality control, policy and practice have been stimulated more often than not by the needs of the military market. It is thus no exaggeration to describe the military as the single most important source of quality improvement. This is remarkable, in that the military is a customer, not a supplier. During the last generation, a great contribution of the military has been to the development and application of quality assurance. This has some important lessons for current applications of quality techniques.

WHY QUALITY FROM MILITARY ACTIVITY?

There appears to be no dominant reason why the military in various countries has been such a demanding and constructive customer, but several factors have played a part. The relationship of the military to the government and the size of the military budget have clearly been important. Official opinions and attitudes can be marshalled readily, and resources devoted to formulating and administering policies towards purchasing. But in neither respect is the military budget unique: at times it may have been the largest customer of all, but other parts of the public sector have on occasion had sufficient size to command attention and compel change among suppliers. One distinction for the military has arisen from the extreme fluctuations in its requirements, between wartime and peacetime. Procedures, systems and equipment have to be able to withstand broader performance criteria than any faced by a civilian organisation, while reliability has to be maintained under the most stressful of conditions. Another distinctive characteristic of military procurement is its frequent need for products that are at the forefront of technological progress. Indeed, on many occasions the military have driven the limits of technical knowledge forward. Other customers have done this too, but the particular combination of conditions facing the armed services has led to an outstanding concern over what the requirements really are and how far they are being met by the goods purchased. Several consequences have inevitably followed, and one of these is a long-standing concern for quality.

For centuries, responsibility for quality in military purchasing was taken by the customer, and the procedures for its implementation were inspection-based. D. G. Spickernell dates the earliest record of inspection to around 1450BC; it is an Egyptian frieze in Thebes, illustrating stone cutting and measurement. The first example in this country, quoted by the Ministry of Defence, is the appointment by King John in 1214 of William Wrotham as Keeper of the King's Ports and Galleys, a post whose duties included the supervision of shipbuilding and repair. In the late seventeenth century, Samuel Pepys, then Secretary to the Admiralty, recorded that overseers had been appointed with direct responsibility for ship construction. Thus there has been a long tradition in the UK whereby the government has had partial or even complete involvement in production facilities, while at the same time retaining the responsibility for quality.

This system lasted until World War I, when increasing variety, rising technical complexity and the sheer volume of wartime purchases strained the abilities of the government inspectors. Accordingly, a condition of contract was introduced in 1916: inspection would be carried out by the manufacturers' staff, with the government's inspectors continuing to examine only a proportion of the deliveries. Something of a stop-gap measure, this nonetheless enabled fewer people to handle much greater quantities of goods, and marked a partial transfer of the responsibility for quality.

THE INSPECTION APPROVED FIRMS SERVICE

Another and more significant innovation around this time came from technical change, for the development of military aircraft posed some unusual quality problems. Design parameters and standards had to be introduced, materials evaluated and construction methods approved, so the Ministry of Supply established its own Aeronautical Inspection Department to handle such matters. As is typical of many new industries based on an emerging technology, the bulk of the manufacture was done by many small producers and subcontractors, so a system of auditing production processes and construction methods was introduced, and there was widespread involvement on questions of design.

Most of the Aeronautical Inspection Department's methods proved to be applicable only to the needs of one armed service. For example, its inspectors are believed to have operated a simple system whereby they either approved something or did not, with no halfway measures. One result of this was that in an attempt to avoid a 'no go' decision, manufacturers tended to over-engineer their products. Of little consequence in aircraft at the time, as questions of safety and performance were paramount, such a detail might have introduced an unacceptable productivity penalty had it been applied to other industries. However, as part of its programme, the department also developed a system by which it inspected and approved the manufacturers' own inspection departments; this, the Inspection Approved Firms Service, or IAFS, was applied widely to military purchasing in the early 1920s.

The IAFS was the main approach to quality control in defence purchasing for five decades. The system worked well, coping adequately with the demanding conditions of World War II, but there were some criticisms. In common with all inspection-based approaches it had a high manning requirement and was prone to the individual errors of the inspectors themselves: although most normally achieve a much higher success rate, anything up to a fifth of inspector decisions may be faulty. So, however it is organised, quality control through inspection alone can lead to a certain level of error, a degree of residual imperfection.

Even if a measure of inspection error could be accepted, there were some other anomalous problems with the IAFS. In placing responsibility for quality on the supplier it tended to focus attention on relatively junior personnel. There was thus no obvious incentive for a contractor's top management to take an interest in quality, and the chief inspector, although nominally reporting to his employers, could in effect find himself directly answerable to the government inspectorate. Such attention might have had, if handled properly, a motivational influence here and there, but any such effect was negated by the practice of the IAFS merely to encourage adequate workmanship to a given specification. The imperfect screen provided by inspection made it more difficult to identify both poor quality and high quality. Inefficiency was thereby concealed.

POLARIS AND QUALITY ASSURANCE

The US military is believed to have adopted a comparable system to the IAFS at around the same time and with similar results. This situation continued until there was a need for radically higher-quality standards in defence equipment and the realisation that inspection-based systems were incapable of delivering them. The 1950s procurement programme which established the watershed for what became known as quality assurance was for the solid-fuel strategic rocket, Polaris, and its associated submarine launch vehicle.

Some of the management implications of the Polaris exercise are well known – for example, how the development of critical path analysis and the early application of computers are said to have saved 18 months of construction time. Less well known are the programme's implications for quality.

In the mid-1950s, Polaris was at the forefront of technical development in several fields: nuclear submarines and their equipment, electronics, solid-fuel rockets, warheads and guidance systems. Furthermore, it involved a fresh combination of technologies and their associated contractors. A very large programme for its time, it required much higher component reliability than had previously been commonplace. With numerous interfaces between technologies and contractors, quality – and the confidence that quality had been developed – were needed at each manufacturing phase.

Traditional methods and approaches were judged to be unsuitable for this task. Instead, a system was designed whereby the contract placed responsibility for quality on the prime contractor, stipulating system requirements while at the same time, the contract-awarding authority made provisions for the approval of the system. Initially the prime contractors' responsibilities extended to the quality produced by their subcontractors, but these were so numerous that it was soon clear that this course was impractical. Accordingly, the purchasing authority arranged to carry out third-party approval of subcontractors, and trained a field force of approvers for this purpose. Thus it was that, through a combination of pressures arising from technical change and expediency, Polaris became, in terms of quality control, the most important programme of the twentieth century.

Success with Polaris led to the production of a quality assurance requirement for US defence suppliers as a whole. Known as MIL-Q-9858A, issued in 1959 and adopted in 1963, this document is unchanged to this day. Its provisions are contract-related and its great strengths, perhaps, are that it is both brief and general. Its basic approach has been followed by subsequent quality assurance standards. It stipulates that:

- there shall be a quality system
- certain posts shall be created in the organisation with responsibility for quality and there shall be certain quality procedures

- documents will be generated at the following stages of the production cycle
- an audit trail will be established for quality matters and someone will follow later to check the system

Such an approach neither states that it guarantees quality nor gives any indication of the nature and scale of any anticipated improvement. It does not say, even on the contract to which it relates, that goods of a certain quality will be supplied but, rather, it starts an organisation (or at least, the division handling the defence contract) on the road to quality assurance. After that, it is up to the organisation itself to improve.

As we can see, MIL-Q-9858A is no cast-iron guarantee of quality: it is possible even to conceive of a situation in which quality assurance has no effect at all on the quality generated. But experience in the USA 30 years ago proved that the chance of this outcome is extremely remote; on the contrary, the system works and works well. The confidence needed to devise such an approach, and the determination required both to apply it to a defence programme of national importance and then to stay with it for several years to prove it worked, must have been of a very high order.

Criticism of quality assurance

Most of the criticism of quality assurance centres on those aspects of the system which were essential to get it started but later appear superfluous and overly bureaucratic. In the literature on quality statements can be found such as this: 'If you want to improve quality, get rid of the quality-control department altogether.' However, it is easy to overlook the role which some of a quality system's attributes now perform in guarding the organisation. They serve as a watchdog against the erosion of standards, and their presence gives the customer confidence that the organisation is indeed selling quality as an integral part of its products. As D. G. Spickernell pointed out, quality is everyone's business and for that very reason there is a danger of it becoming nobody's business. The quality department is there to see this does not happen.

Polaris in the UK

The Polaris system was purchased by the UK in 1962 and with it came provisions for contract-related procurement quality assurance. A much smaller project in the UK, with four rather than the USA's 41 submarines built, it was still a very large undertaking for the Ministry of Defence. Completed on time and on cost, some of the credit for this achievement is attributed to the naval officer in charge, Vice-Admiral Sir Rufus Mackenzie, and to the director of the associated technical programme, Sir Rowland Baker. A contract document was produced defining quality procedures along US lines; this was known as 'General Requirements for the Assurance of Quality (Submarines)', or GRAQS. Based on this, a similar quality procedure was produced for surface ships a couple of years later, in 1965: 'Standard Conditions for Inspections and Tests', or SCITS. Despite its name, this was very much a quality control document and, together with GRAQS, led to radical change in the Royal Navy's overseeing service. Accordingly, a new post was created to handle the reorganisation and help introduce the new quality assurance concepts. The first holder of this post was Captain D. G. (Spike) Spickernell.

DEVELOPMENT OF QUALITY ASSURANCE IN THE UK

By 1960 some of the limitations of the IAFS had been widely recognised in the UK, and it was appreciated in several areas of industry and the armed services that quality and reliability would have to get better. Various methods to improve the situation were tried, such as the more intensive use of practical quality techniques, notably SPC and reliability testing. In a similar approach to that of the IAFS, there was also an attempt to introduce a system for design approval. Valuable though some of these contributions undoubtedly were, their effects were localised and piecemeal and they failed to address a principal shortcoming of the IAFS: the lack of attention to quality by top management.

AVIATION PUBLICATION 92

One line of development towards a comprehensive quality system which would be of concern to top management came, like the IAFS nearly 50 years before, from the Aircraft Inspection Department. The Ministry of Supply had, in 1965, taken on additional responsibilities and become the Ministry of Technology, an organisation which, while its interests included defence, was separate from the Ministry of Defence. It produced a document known as Aviation Publication 92, or AvP 92: 'Specification of Quality Management Requirements'. Issued in 1968, AvP 92, like GRAQS and SCITS a few years earlier, transferred responsibility for both final quality and purchased inputs away from the purchaser to the prime contactor. But, also like the naval documents, AvP 92 catered for the specialised needs of one armed service. Aircraft production had by now been concentrated into a few hands, unlike the position in the 1920s, so that even if electronics systems and equipment were included there would have been only a score or so of major prime contractors, all of whom had long experience in the defence market. Measures which might be suitable in such a context would not necessarily be so elsewhere.

THE MENSFORTH AND RABY REPORTS

To find a way forward, the government appointed two committees, one chaired by Colonel Raby, to examine quality in the military domain, and the other under Sir Eric Mensforth, to recommend measures for wider civilian applications. Both committees reported, but a sustained civilian initiative was not achieved at first. This illustrates the importance, at a crucial point in the application of quality assurance, of a very large organisation, with resources and market authority, to grasp the quality assurance concept and then advance it. The Ministry of Defence was able to provide such a lead, so the Raby report is the one which is remembered.

The Raby report effectively endorsed the quality procedures which the Royal Navy had been following for the previous five years.

Responsibility for quality was to be transferred from the customer to the supplier yet quality was to remain market-orientated; it was to centre on what mattered to the customer. Furthermore, although a relatively narrow definition of quality was adopted – conformance to specification – its generation was seen as a management function. Quality, according to the report, is determined where work is done and the control of quality is the control of work and assurance of quality comes from evidence that all necessary work has been done properly.

Another vital conclusion of the Raby Committee was that the technical competence of potential contractors should be evaluated before defence contracts are let and that these contractors should have adequate quality arrangements. Seemingly innocuous, this condition advocated a move away from contract-related quality assurance to the quality assurance of the whole organisation, a vastly greater under-taking for nearly all contractors. Experience had proved that, contrary to expectations, the effects of contract-related conditions did not in fact disseminate rapidly around a firm. The effects in the two prime contractors for the UK Polaris programme, Vickers and Cammell Laird, could have been observed at the time: both had widely differing pertaining conditions between the divisions producing submarines and those departments engaged on a variety of other defence and civilian business.

The years after the appearance of the Raby report saw the reorganisation of purchasing and quality authorities in the public sector. Within the Ministry of Defence the various quality inspector-ates were first, in 1970, restyled 'Quality Assurance Directorates' and then placed under the control of a new purchasing administration, the Procurement Executive, which was being formed under a seconded business executive, Derek (now Lord) Rayner. These defence quality interests were then unified into the Defence Quality Assurance Board, DQAB, and a new industry liaison committee was formed to advise it, the Defence Industries Quality Assurance Panel, or DIQAP. These were events of outstanding significance for quality, for at last the Ministry of Defence was presenting a united front to industry on quality issues. Its authority and credibility rose accordingly.

In 1969 the Raby report had noted that there were 16,500 personnel in the Ministry of Defence working on quality issues, nearly all of them inspectors. An early priority of Derek Rayner's was to reduce greatly this number through implementing the Raby Report. The naval documents GRAQS and SCITS and the Ministry of Technology's AvP 92 already existed, but all were contract-related and specialised. Furthermore, there was evidently a major task ahead in getting any of these systems accepted widely. The styles of GRAQS, SCITS and AvP 92 were such that the documents were essentially telling a potential supplier what to do and how to organise, and it was thought that this might complicate their acceptance. Happily, an alternative was to hand from the North Atlantic Treaty Organisation, or NATO.

QUALITY DEVELOPMENT AT NATO

Quality problems had been widespread in NATO in the 1950s. The recognition that there were differing traditions, standards and requirements between the members, coupled with the rise of cross-border purchasing, led to some work on standardisation and quality, starting in 1961. Thereafter, from 1965, efforts were redirected towards a common NATO quality assurance policy, with the principal contributions coming from the USA and UK. This initiative led to a document known as 'Standardisation Agreement 4107', which provided, among other things, for a National Quality Assurance Authority in the supplying country to undertake quality assurance free of charge for the purchasing country in cross-border defence deals. Transferring responsibility from buyer to seller thus became part of a NATO agreement, and a series of quality documents – the 'Allied Quality Assurance Publications' (AQAPs) – had to be prepared to back it. The first of these appeared in 1968, the remainder following over the next two years. AQAPs had to be sufficiently general and acceptable to apply anywhere within the NATO member countries. Although conceived and used as contractual documents, they were not related to the needs of any one production sector or armed service, and so could be used as standards against which companies could be assessed prior to the placement of contracts.

Defence Standards 05 series

The Ministry of Defence adopted the AQAPs and republished them, with a few additions, in April 1973 as the 'Defence Standards 05' series. The amendments mostly concerned a stronger emphasis on design, for a system which was to have a profound effect on industrial policy. Implementation was clearly going to be a great hurdle; major defence contractors already renowned for their quality indicated at the outset that it would take about a year to comply with the 'Defence Standards 05' series, to say nothing of going out and approving their subcontractors. With the possibility that the programme might extend way into the future, rapid acceptance of quality assurance required a third party to guide and handle the assessment and approval of companies, just as the Americans had found with Polaris 15 years before. The Ministry of Defence was the only agency with the resources and motivation to undertake this at short notice. Thus, having transferred prospective responsibility for quality to its suppliers, the Ministry took a step back towards industrial participation with third party assessments.

A training programme was devised for all the assessors, and about 1,000 inspectors were put through it. Teams were then assembled which had sufficient technical expertise to be able to relate quality assurance to the sector and the products of the companies to which they were assigned. By 1979, 3,000 companies had been approved and a list of assessed contractors, LAC, produced. Only about one-fifth of UK manufacturing is involved wholly or partially with the defence market, yet in 1979 the number of firms outside the LAC with a quality system was only about 20, of whom most based their procedures on BS5179, itself a product of military practice.

Following the appearance of BS5750 in 1979, the pace of third party quality assurance and approval has increasingly been set by civilian agencies. In 1981, the Ministry of Defence reached agreement with the British Standards Institution that third party assessment against BS5750 was to be considered equal to Ministry of Defence assessment for defence subcontracting. From 1987, the Ministry of Defence no longer assessed firms solely engaged on subcontract work, although continuing to assess all prime contractors. It is possible that in future the Ministry will give up all certification and approval activity adequately covered by other parties, but this will depend on the depth, scope and thoroughness of the assessment process, since the Ministry of Defence typically allocates significantly more time to each company than some other certifiers. Many of the differences in this respect have been greatly reduced in recent years and a consistent approach has been promoted by, notably, the National Accreditation Council for Certification Bodies, or NACCB. But the issue is unlikely to be far away as the process of certification makes inroads among small companies.

Today the Ministry of Defence is increasingly using NATO documents on industrial matters that are directly appropriate to its needs. NATO's efforts on quality assurance are principally to gain acceptance for the 'ISO 9000' series among all its members, and clearly this implies only some very minor amendments, if any, to the Ministry of Defence's quality assurance procedures. However, a partial reversion to procurement quality assurance, seen recently in the amended AQAP 1, could reflect an attempt to secure rapid acceptance of the quality assurance principle in countries less advanced in these matters than the UK.

With quality assurance established in the UK, it may be questioned whether the pattern of defence procurement has reached an ultimate state. But, although there is no sign of any radical change in the foreseeable future, this would seem unlikely. In particular, it may be noted that the characteristics which historically associated defence procurement with quality are still around. Technologies move on, weapons and equipment change, and production methods evolve; against such a background, it is premature to think that the division of responsibility for quality issues and the extent to which the Ministry of Defence works with its suppliers could ever be completely stable. Defence quality assurance is, after all, about the degree of confidence the customer has in the quality of the products purchased. Raise or lower that confidence level, and the measures taken to achieve it might likewise need to be adjusted. Besides, the quality received by the Ministry of Defence is influenced by other measures, for designs, specifications and requirements are subject to a variety of degrees of direct and indirect participation. It may be doubted whether the pattern of customer activity in these areas could ever be fixed.

QUALITY ASSURANCE EVALUATED

How successful has quality assurance been for military purchasing? In terms of the reduction in the resources devoted to quality issues, outstandingly so. There were 16,500 quality personnel employed in 1969, around 5,000 in 1975, 3,500 in 1985 and 2,700 in 1989. One of the original aims of the Procurement Executive has thus been met in full.

The accompanying improvement in quality is more difficult to assess, since no formal attempt has been made to evaluate it and much of the information on defence suppliers is restricted for security reasons. However, a general opinion is that it has improved markedly. Examine the progress of companies which applied quality assurance in the 1970s and you find that those which accepted the principle most enthusiastically have subsequently tended to be the most successful.

Two questions for history

The UK successfully developed quality assurance from procurement quality assurance and then proceeded to be the first country with a widespread civilian system. In such circumstances it might seem surprising that some stages of development were not seen very much earlier. After all, there was little new in the elements of quality assurance. Suppliers had for a long time been required to have certain responsibilities, and to utilise relevant systems and procedures, while the concept of third party certification had existed for centuries with the craft guilds. If all that was new was a fresh combination of factors and purposes, why could not the Aircraft Inspection Department have produced something similar to AvP 92 in the late 1920s, rather than 40 years later? The answer seems to be that the Aircraft Inspection Department was aiming for structural integrity, as opposed to quality, and its methods were inspection-based. Introducing quality assurance requires re-allocations of skills, procedures and jobs – all of which are large steps for inspectors to take.

Another intriguing question concerning the development of quality assurance is this: why did the USA not go beyond procurement quality assurance to produce a general civilian system? It seems that the Americans considered that either coercion or a substantial inducement, such as a large contract, was essential to gain acceptance for quality assurance. As it was, scepticism was expressed over the Ministry of Defence's chances of achieving successful compliance with their programme in the 1970s. Exactly why some US civilian agency did not pick up the idea of quality assurance around, say, 1960 is far from clear, but the fragmentation of standards institutes could be a factor. Today, there are about 1,400 bodies publishing standards in the USA, of which perhaps 10 are broadly comparable to BSI. Introduction of such a huge programme as quality assurance needed a level of authority which it seems none of these bodies have had. (There is a representative grouping, but this was created for US participation in international standards.) Quality assurance was advanced in the civilian domain by the Apollo project to put a man on the moon, and the measures are believed to have been contract-related.

These points put a perspective on the Ministry of Defence's achievement, for a substantial example was necessary before a civilian programme could be sustained. The Mensforth Report of 1969 had failed directly to stimulate civilian quality assurance and it was not until the mid-1970s that the necessary commitment was made and BS5750 was developed. This followed the appearance of a report (issued by the NEDO) from Sir Frederick Warner and the move of the Head of the Defence Quality Assurance Board, Rear-Admiral D. G. Spickernell, to BSI, firstly as its Technical Director and later as its Director General. By that time, quality assurance had a track record.

7
Towards total quality

SYNERGY

The concept of synergy – that the whole can be greater than the sum of the parts – was widely advocated as a source of strategic gain about a generation ago, but examples of it working exactly as it was intended to were hard to find. Sometimes described as 'two plus two equals five', the idea of synergy in industry referred to the gains supposed to come from combining interests and applying good management through planning methods. Exactly how synergy was to work in this context was obscure and the idea came to be discredited.

When implementing quality, however, perhaps the most important aspect to grasp is that synergy *works*. But the synergy is between the techniques and the overall scale of the effort, rather than between activities and pieces of organisations, as strategic planning once viewed it. There is though, a similarity in that results are disproportionate to the amount of effort put in towards quality. Indeed, the concept works so well that, if it is turned round, it implies that the features generating quality will do little on their own. Take any aspect of a quality programme and it is not difficult to find examples of disappointments:

- quality circles which were implemented only after painstaking trouble, but which achieved little and eventually came apart

- zero-defects programmes which were isolated, ill conceived measures with few lasting results
- marketing studies, research efforts and major design initiatives which may have made substantial contributions but failed to lead to a sustained improvement in quality

Occasionally, it may even have been better if the technique in question had not been tried. Determined quality-improvement drives lead towards a state of total quality (or company-wide quality control, as it is called in Japan), whereas isolated measures fail.

TOTAL QUALITY

Total quality is the achievement of quality through every aspect of an organisation capable of making a contribution towards it. It does not represent an ultimate state of quality – there is always room for improvement – but instead it aims to produce the best it can with contributions from operations, marketing, design, specific 'quality techniques' and, perhaps above all, from *people*. Everyone involved should be attuned to the goal of ever-increasing quality. Operatives, supervisors, middle managers and higher management; all should know what they can do to contribute, how to do it and have the motivation to carry it out. Total quality is thus likely to be more than an assembly of constituent features, since it will condition the organisational culture.

Exactly how much will need to be done and how much time will be required to take an organisation through to total quality depends partly on its condition at the outset. Traditions, skills and structures differ between organisations – and between countries: the way used successfully in one place may not necessarily be the best approach elsewhere. What has been proved right for Japan, for instance, need not be the best way forward in the USA. Even though there is still far to go, particularly among smaller and medium-sized organisations, quality is improving in the UK. Consequently, there will probably be something to build on and develop.

QUALITY AS A STRATEGIC AIM

The first step towards total quality is probably the same anywhere and the fact that it needs to be mentioned at all is a sorry commentary on the status of quality issues. It is the acceptance of the principle of total quality at the highest level. The need for quality, and its benefits, are obvious. However, the costs involved and the timescale for implementation may be difficult to accept. With most programmes extending over a matter of years and little likelihood of early returns, it may be hard to accept utilitarian arguments for quality. Yes, the returns greatly outweigh the costs and yes, quality is an essential precondition for longer-term survival, but if there are substantial costs at first and virtually no returns for a couple of years, some other priorities may have to be considered. A degree of leader's vision is needed to accept the implications of total quality, so in many organisations, commitment must be at the top.

Once the idea of quality has been adopted as a strategic aim, the process – probably a long one – of conditioning attitudes throughout the organisation should be started. The notion should be established that *everyone* is into the quality programme for the long term. This should be associated with visible commitments to the longer-term features of the research, design and marketing programmes on a scale which the prospective results can withstand.

QUALITY ASSURANCE

In the UK the route to total quality has quality assurance as a key feature. A few references use the term 'quality assurance' in place of 'quality control'; here, by 'quality assurance', we mean the compliance with a standard for a quality system which is laid down externally and inspected. This has been the major quality development in the UK over the last generation. It will not guarantee that quality follows, and results depend on the enthusiasm with which it is taken up and applied. There can be a vast difference between what is done for some of its provisions to achieve certification and what otherwise could be possible. But, if accepted and implemented, it

introduces any organisation to so much of total quality and in
sufficient depth that appropriate determination will lead to sustained
quality improvements. Once quality has been fully accepted as a
strategic aim, an early start should be made on introducing a quality
assurance standard.

PROGRESS BY STEPS OR LEAPS?

As implementation proceeds and the results start coming through,
their initial trend is likely to be towards perfection within the
original context of the status quo. Their emphasis will be towards
doing things right and at this stage, there may well be scope for
achieving radically higher conformance to specifications in a short
space of time. P. B. Crosby terms this a 'quantum leap' of progress;
this is the same or very similar to J. M. Juran's concept of 'breakthrough' (see page 24) – that is, an organisation demanding of itself
not just an incremental improvement but progress of a different
order. This may be triggered by setting zero defects as a management
standard or by demanding that things be 'done right first time'.
Whatever the terminology, it will imply quite clearly to all that only
the best is good enough. Through spurring attitudes and a rapid
reassessment of the methods whereby standards are met, a great leap
forward is accomplished. People are now doing the right things and
they know it; progress has occurred in such a short space of time that
it is self-evident and this, too, provides widespread encouragement.

However, success with such methods appears to have created some
misunderstandings over the nature of the quality-improvement process. A notable misapprehension is that progress should necessarily
be attained through a few, very large steps. In practice, such a leap-
forward is likely to be a once-and-for-all phase. Its mechanism is not
entirely clear, but a major part of the story appears to be the
resistance to change which can build up virtually anywhere. Demand
urgency against a clear target and there will not be the time for
restrictive practices to develop. The mere scope for such an improvement indicates there has been no long standing total quality programme. With a pattern of little historic change, bureaucratic

practices and the presence of much middle management indicate potential for substantial improvement.

Incremental improvements

As the quality programme proceeds, operations work more efficiently and to a higher specification, suppliers are encouraged to produce what is wanted to a closer timetable, design improves and contributes to quality and reliability, and marketing becomes more accurate, reflecting changing preferences more rapidly. It then becomes possible to simplify the organisation's systems. The main reason why systems ever became complicated was that the information flows involved too many managers and elaborate internal control. Now it should be possible to shorten and smooth the paths of communication.

Once an organisation has been adapted and attuned to total quality and the quality techniques have been put in, the maintenance of quality and further incremental gains involve leadership, motivation and personnel. Quality is then seen to be about people – how they are organised and motivated, the corporate culture they have to work in, and the attitudes encouraged in them by the idea of total quality. Quality is also about who is hired and how they are trained. It is an unending process.

Training and education

At worst, training can be an essential but limited precondition for the rudiments of quality techniques to be covered. If that is all it amounts to, it will be a low-status activity with a dismal image, and the opportunities it presents will have been lost. If, instead, the training programme is conducted imaginatively and comprehensively, it may be turned into the driving force behind a quality campaign.

A training programme should create interest in quality for nearly everyone in the organisation. It should lead to direct and active involvement in quality issues and to the acceptance of the idea of total quality. Implementation will be greatly assisted once everyone accepts that following the quality path is a good idea and knows what is to be done, how, and by whom. Such an educational programme will be sufficiently thorough as to reflect the prior commitment to total quality at the highest level.

Organisational needs assessment

Educational programmes have much in common, but the differences are sufficiently wide that each has to be tailored to the particular needs of the situation in hand. In order to isolate these needs, a broad-based task group, drawn not just from the personnel and training departments, should be set up. The investigation should proceed in two stages, the first covering what the organisation requires for total quality. This need should be evaluated broadly in relation to its culture, activities, suppliers, markets, customers and the nature of its systems. An outline should then be made of what changes will be needed for total quality and the ease with which they can be introduced.

Personnel needs assessment

Once a profile of corporate requirements has been prepared, it becomes possible to assess how far they are being met already by current personnel. This second phase of the exercise will almost certainly be the easier one, if only because nearly all available training assessments concentrate on people rather than organisations.

A balance of two approaches is typically necessary. On the one hand, the core of long-term employees, the people who are making their careers within the organisation and identify strongly with it, can be isolated; what do they now need to develop their careers within a total-quality culture? The other approach is to see what expertise is already available and how it is spread around the structure. Relating abilities to levels in the hierarchy then discloses a pattern of deficiencies by seniority. Both approaches are open to criticism when used on their own, so a combination is likely to be mandatory.

The training programme

Having analysed the training needs, the educational programme can be put together. Once total quality has been established, it may be possible to provide ongoing training at just two levels: the shop floor and higher management. However, at first (particularly in larger organisations) it may be necessary to stream the programme in several ways, for instance:

* top management
* middle management
* supervisors
* shop floor

The prospective programme is then divided up as appropriate, everything being covered in outline at the top, and as much content as people can take at the bottom. The overall programme is likely to include:

* what quality is, why it is worth attaining and how it is defined in the organisation
* how a total-quality system differs from traditional practice
* why everyone has to be involved and support the new initiative
* duties of each hierarchy level
* techniques for selecting, gathering, organising and using data
* simple approaches to problem solving
* the role of suppliers and operations
* design – marketing, engineering and industrial design
* Statistical Process Control (SPC)
* how the total-quality programme is to proceed

While education is essential if the applied techniques are to be put into the hands of those who will use them, there is a danger that an undue emphasis will be placed on a set of skills to be used mostly at a junior level; this applies particularly where the programme is organised on a competency basis. If you have little discretion over the content of a programme, try to orientate the course material towards actual problems, preferably from within the organisation, rather than to a set of techniques that might have a more general application.

Sources of resistance

Two widespread difficulties a total-quality programme is likely to encounter are:

- disbelief in the potential for quality
- resistance to change

Education should be able to answer the first of these. People think that they are already doing what is necessary for quality, and wonder what changes could possibly be made. The short answer is that they are not actually being asked to do much which is different and, in particular, that total quality does not mean working harder than before. Rather, as W. E. Deming puts it, people will be working smarter, not harder!

The second difficulty is less easy to tackle, and may be the principle reason why quality is in its current state. This is the resistance to training – and to change of any sort – seen in nearly all organisations, and typically among middle management. Gaining support and participation from those who see their positions as threatened is essential, and it is a primary responsibility of top management to secure it.

8

John Makepeace's workshop and the Parnham Trust

CRAFTSMANSHIP

Parnham House, a grade one listed historic building in West Dorset, is the home of John Makepeace, the furniture designer. There, too, is his workshop, where a team of eight craftsmen produces furniture to the highest standards. The building also houses the Parnham Trust, which since 1977 has run the School for Craftsmen in Wood, providing a two-year course for 22 students in design, cabinetmaking and enterprise management. The Parnham Trust's latest venture is at Hooke Park, a 134-hectare (330-acre) woodland situated 5km (three miles) from Parnham. The Hooke Park College for Advanced Manufacturing in Wood is being established there to develop and teach young entrepreneurs the technologies required to use sustainable but neglected resources of timber in manufacturing. The first 12 students started this two-year course at Easter 1989.

Examples of fine craftsmanship exist from almost every age. Indeed, such a profusion of collectors' pieces survive that sometimes it seems as though there was once a Golden Age for quality, which passed with the onset of the Industrial Revolution, mechanisation and the rise of production in large factories. Whether such quality would have been recognised widely at the time can be seriously questioned. The population was far smaller, there were fewer goods of all kinds for each person, and many – possibly most – of these would have been produced to no better than a rudimentary standard. Very fine craftsmanship may thus have been confined to the market created by the elite. Furthermore, it is easy to observe the products of numerous times – the swords of Damascus and Japan, the armour of Milan and Nuremberg, the furniture of eighteenth-century Paris – and forget that quality has been achieved typically only in isolated centres and for a certain period. Lacking today's communications, it is even less likely that quality was readily and widely apparent; that said, it did exist, and was produced in workshops run by master craftsmen with a skill-based hierarchy. As industrialisation helped erode the former craft structure, output may have risen, but something was lost.

The decline of the old craft customs and standards differed between countries and sectors. In Germany and Switzerland, for example, a strong tradition of master and apprentice is widely retained today. A combination of formal and informal methods, centred on personal relationships and tasks at the workplace, helps to promote some high technical standards in these countries (though they are open to the criticism of being light on innovation and design flair). Many direct comparisons between countries and different ages should be made with caution, for conditions and contexts may vary in important if almost imperceptible ways. But the re-establishment of some of the former traditions and values has a contribution to make in the UK today. In taking John Makepeace's workshop and school as an example, parallels may be drawn with historic forebears over size, geographical isolation, markets, standards and the innovation developed.

QUALITY THROUGH CRAFTSMANSHIP AND DESIGN

John Makepeace spotted quality in furniture at an early age, aspired to achieve it, and then faced the problem of how to obtain access to the necessary standards for its production. Evidently, craftsmanship was needed. This, too, came early, but something more would be needed for a successful commercial operation. If John Makepeace was to have a worthwhile career, high standards and quality would have to be essential; they were of such importance that they became a matter of ethics. There just had to be a practical way for ethics, and so John Makepeace was led into design.

Views can differ over the scope of design and at Parnham it is interpreted broadly. Design describes and specifies a piece to be produced: for this it must express what is happening in the market-place and must understand the context of the market. It then defines the customer's need and discovers a solution to it. Substantially overlapping with marketing, design becomes a means of establishing common ground with clients once initial contact has been made. So a design initially gravitates towards what the market wants, yet a dialogue starts with the designer which takes the client into new territory, drives the market forward, and paves the way for an innovative solution.

Although the customer is of great importance, there are other critical influences, notably those factors determining the workshop's ability to produce a piece. Capacity, a technical issue in a factory, is more of a human problem in a small workshop; in particular, the designer has to think of the capabilities and personal development of individual craftsmen. Produce too many simple items and there can be the danger of excessive repetition, yet, on the other hand, there are dangers, too, from undue pressure. Huge personal stresses can build up for a craftsman on a major piece, so complexity must be related to ability. Careful assessment of what people can handle is thus an important part of the design process.

Location and quality

John Makepeace started his workshop at Banbury in the 1960s and initially found that a lot of people could not understand that quality mattered. Eventually, though, they were persuaded. The move to Parnham House came in 1976, and it raised the whole tenor of the business. There was the immediate practical effect of having larger and better workshops. The attractions of the house and its grounds as a place to work made it easier to obtain good staff, despite the rural location in West Dorset. Public awareness and perception changed, too: more was expected, and the staff rose to the challenge. Subsequently Parnham has generated an even greater stimulus for those working there, as several aspects of its organisation have been built up, each becoming a mutual source of strength. A permanent exhibition of work displays the products in an appropriate setting so that, for example, students of the School for Craftsmen in Wood see a separate yet closely related business and are inspired by it. Pervading everything is the intangible air of success. Quality is apparent everywhere; and the customers likewise see it and relate to it.

Surroundings are another major factor at Hooke Park. At the time of the estate's acquisition from the Forestry Commission in 1982, much needed to be done. Mostly planted just over a generation ago, the trees had been largely neglected over the intervening years. Among the Parnham Trust's aims was to raise the quality of the timber produced through the application of better forestry management; this also had the effect of improving the environment for those who were later to work there. Innovative buildings have subsequently been commissioned to house the Hooke Park College, which makes substantial use of the local timber. Set in woodland and bringing together educational, research and production facilities, the location provides outstanding inspiration for a course on entrepreneurship and design with a rural emphasis.

Leadership and motivation

Parnham creates an inherent culture, and there is the social sense of a common goal, but a strong personal lead comes from John Makepeace himself. The closest direction is given to the workshop, encouraging, challenging, and if necessary pressuring the craftsmen. They are all specialists, and so the leader has to cover every field. Leadership comes primarily from the principal and the design tutor, so John Makepeace's relationship towards the students is more detached. Although the style of the school is open, a clear purpose is provided, and this enables a degree of formality to be set and maintained. The intensive, multidisciplinary programme is similar to that found in many small businesses. Self-reliance is necessary in a number of the disciplines commonly taught in isolation from one another.

Mechanisation and suppliers

In a labour-intensive activity such as Parnham's furniture production, it is interesting to note that traditional working methods do not appear to be followed for their own sake. Mechanised processes are available, and can bring some important benefits. The craftsman's aim is to concentrate his or her skills on improving the product; if mechanisation helps in this, so much the better.

Supplies form a relatively minor part of the picture at Parnham. Certain metal components are bought-in, and there is some scope here for working towards outstanding quality. Likewise, timber has to be purchased, and there is a search for unusual items. But most of the value added in the final product is applied at Parnham itself. Hooke Park College has, as one of its objectives, the development of uses of indigenous timber, much of it in the form of woodland thinnings which would otherwise have been wasted. Developing supplies is thus a part of Parnham's strategy.

Quality and commercial pressures

Certain conflicts between quality and financial returns can arise in the workshop. The danger of excessive repetition for the craftsmen (as already mentioned) and, naturally, its avoidance can lead to a commercial trade-off. Repetition may also compromise quality which, being based partly on innovative design, requires continual repositioning in a changing market. Innovation and the quest for quality drive the business, and so the path followed in the future may not necessarily be quite the same as that of the past. As this could have financial implications in the near term, the outlook and objectives have to be set firmly in the longer-term future if total quality is to be attained at Parnham.

John Makepeace sets out to achieve quality, to ally design with craftsmanship, to work closely with customers through a system of patronage, and to run his organisation so as to develop its members. It is likely that all of these conditions pertained in the master craftsmens' workshops of previous centuries.

9
Nimbus Records

BACKGROUND

Nimbus Records is the largest manufacturer in the UK of compact discs, or CDs, and has a very high reputation for quality. Most of its turnover of around £26.5M in the year to March 31st 1990 involved mastering and pressing recordings from other music companies. However, the organisation also has recording facilities and its own record label, which provide about a tenth of sales and take a rather smaller proportion of the discs pressed.

Although the company was incorporated in 1971, the business had been started a few years earlier; it was based in Birmingham and recorded classical music. Its founder and current president, Count Numa Labinsky, was a singer with an entrepreneurial career that started immediately after his arrival in England from France in June 1940. His business activities had included, for a time in the 1950s, the production of recorded music. Nimbus was started with two co-directors, Michael Reynolds, an electrical engineer, and his brother, Gerald Reynolds. Some property interests were also brought in; at times during those early years, these formed the greater part of the business. Headquarters moved from Birmingham to the current location, a country house called Wyastone Leys, near Monmouth, in 1975 and 18 months later the pressing of LP vinyl discs started there too. It was still quite a small operation, although by 1984 sales of LPs rose to about £0.5M. Rationalising these events in the light of hindsight, it would seem as though it took the company 17½ years to get established.

A major strategic turning point came in 1982, with the prospect of the CD as a rival to LPs. Nimbus decided it had to be in this new market and, by 1984, had become the second company in Europe after Philips (Polygram) to be producing CDs. Output expanded greatly, and a new production facility was instigated at Cwmbran in 1986, while another, at Charlottesville, Virginia, came the following year. Each of these plants now employs around 250 people.

A passion for music and its reproduction has been perhaps the outstanding driving force for quality at Nimbus. For its own label, the company has specialised almost entirely in classical music, which, with its wider dynamic range than that of other music forms, makes greater demands on recording and reproduction equipment. The standards achieved could be assessed readily against actual performances, so helping to promote the drive for ever-closer degrees of perfection. Somehow Nimbus had to raise disc quality to get its recordings across.

The Nimbus house style in music production under its Music Director, Adrian Farmer, is to promote artistic communication by interfering as little as possible. The scene is set at Wyastone Leys and the surroundings provided are notably more stimulating than those at some of the urban recording studios. Long 'takes' and minimal editing provide their own disciplines, while technical stages between the microphone and the final product are reduced as far as possible for the CD format. That is the house style; and from there it is up to the artists.

QUALITY, SERVICE AND DELIVERY

Product quality was achieved at Nimbus in the early days and word about it spread informally among the music companies, the major customers, although other aspects of quality (notably customer service and delivery) were at this time decidedly open to criticism. However, the market's requirements were far less exacting than those of today (for example, delivery lead times could be 5-6 weeks, whereas now they can be just a few days). Nonetheless, a business manager was needed and one was found in Mike Lee, who joined the company in 1976 and remained on the board until his death in 1987. He set a standard on an aspect of the organisation's operations and then saw that it was met.

QUALITY THROUGH TECHNICAL BRILLIANCE

Nimbus's technical and design capabilities were instrumental in achieving product quality and paving the way for expansion over the five years to 1989. Having decided to get into CD production in 1982, the clear route was to buy a disc-mastering system from either Philips or Sony. However, the price of a single machine from either supplier, around £2M, was a very large investment indeed at the time for a company of Nimbus's size. Furthermore, there were some technical objections, and so it was decided to develop Nimbus's own laser mastering system from patents licensed from Philips. The daunting task of improving on the research effort of a large corporation in a field of technical progress will be recognised by many medium-sized organisations. Confidence was important. A Nimbus party had been shown around the research laboratory of one electronics multinational which had a vast array of costly-looking equipment, but gradually it was realised that little of this was likely to have been applied to any one project. Thus, with suitable concentration on the chosen field, Nimbus's resources and manpower proved adequate for the company's intentions.

Dr Jonathan Halliday, now on the board, was taken on as head of research. Within 10 months a technically superior disc-mastering system had been produced (in 1983) for about one-eighth of the cost of buying it in. Subsequently there have been improvements to product quality through refinements to various production processes, as well as through some automation. Both costs and reject rates have fallen.

QUALITY AND CHANGE

Technical advance and innovation are now likely to lead to further diversification at Nimbus. A substantial increase in the capacity of CDs – a development in which the company leads – has now created a commercial-length disc for video applications, and the prospect is that these can also be used for enlarged computer read-only memories (ROMs). Already, CDs with a much higher storage density than those currently used for music can store *all* UK telephone directories on a single disc. Combinations of information, video and music are possible and clearly, the potential applications for these higher densities are enormous. Market development is, however, dependent on standards set for the sector and on the availability of complementary reproduction equipment. Inevitably, much depends on the decisions of larger organisations.

QUALITY TO THE FINAL CUSTOMER

The customer's view of quality in a CD hinges partly on the sound it produces. Although open to a measure of subjective judgement, standards here are largely a technical matter which may be assessed through technical processes. Philips issued a standard with its patents for the error rate in recorded information, but this was far too high. Nimbus operates to a rejection limit four times better than the Philips threshold, and a typical production run achieves 10-14 times better.

Customer satisfaction also depends on largely subjective matters such as the quality of the print on the label and the finish of the lacquer. A majority of rejects are for these reasons; the company decides its standards, and it can be a moot issue whether they should be raised or lowered. Having its own record label enables Nimbus to assess closely the market's tastes, views and preferences.

MARKETING

Recorded music is a difficult market in which to operate. Final demand is dependent principally on discretionary income, there is a strong seasonal component, and the market's dynamics are complicated. With, for most of its output, three stages of distribution between Nimbus and the final consumer, any of several sources of competitive pressure can be brought to bear on the organisation's price and volume. Furthermore, there can be difficulties in getting quality recognised as a competitive feature, as happens when a customer orders a couple of thousand discs, distributes the review copies from this batch and then places the balance of production quantities elsewhere at a cheaper price. On the other hand, customer loyalty is a significant factor, with a long-standing reputation for quality reinforcing current standards. Actual market intelligence is through both formal and informal processes.

Corporate culture and structure

There has been no conscious attempt to steer the corporate culture at Nimbus. A combination of circumstances, history and the influence of the leading personalities has moulded what happens to be there. Continuity and a sense of stability from the executive directors have played a part, but the dominant characteristics have come from the structure and style of management chosen. Structure is low and flat – there are, essentially, no middle managers; a group of perhaps four key personnel run each of the two factories, but the view from headquarters is of separate, parallel production units, with considerable autonomy, rather than closely controlled plants run by local middle managers. Geographical separation plays a part here, too. From the shopfloor, looking upwards, there is no intervening managerial barrier between either the factory management or the central group of directors. Communications are excellent, and an open-door policy is operated. Anyone at all can contact a director at any time about any problem.

Personnel and training

Nimbus's structure, coupled with this effort to remove barriers, greatly influences patterns of work. Individuals have their principal tasks and an area of affinity, but are encouraged to move beyond this as necessary and, on occasion, may be required to do so. Some functions are more important and difficult to replace than others but, even with this limitation, a considerable amount of job rotation occurs. Group cooperation emerges informally and is encouraged. Groups compare their relative performances and differences between shifts; they could be seen as informal quality circles, but are not so called. Everyone in the core team of the permanent staff identifies with the idea of quality. Workforce turnover is low and training is given as needed. Some posts require little or none, and this makes a seasonal workforce possible. Others need much. As a result of these differences, averages for the time and effort entailed for training are not meaningful.

PROCESS CONTROL

Until recently, Nimbus inspected visually every disc to be sold. A machine now carries out technical inspection, with samples taken from every run for further visual inspection. Statistical returns from production are analysed informally; there are neither so many machines nor so many processes that the norms for performance cannot be established readily and memorised by whoever is reviewing the system. Inevitably, reactions from headquarters to these figures will always be slower than the immediate response on the shop floor could be, so a roving quality inspector has been appointed at each plant whose job is to identify problems at source or as they occur.

QUALITY AND THE NEXT PROFIT AND LOSS ACCOUNT

Quality to the customer is held constant – if it drops, everyone shouts – but the reject rate at Nimbus does fluctuate, most notably so when output was expanded a couple of years ago. Naturally, there can be times when there is a direct trade-off between quality and the prospective returns. Why not lower quality temporarily and raise profits? Why not pass through to sales some of those rejects which have minor print defects but fully satisfactory music? It is not quite the company's style to do so, although anyone concerned predominantly with the *next* results might be tempted to lower standards.

Quality might be hard to defend if financial issues were the only pressures and conversely, maintaining a quality ethos requires a view extending further than the next set of accounts. Such an attitude is to be found at Nimbus Records. Nimbus have found that concentration on quality leads to improved yields.

10

The National Trust

IDENTIFYING QUALITY IN SERVICE ORGANISATIONS

Service organisations that are developing quality are hard to select, partly because quality is more difficult to define in this field. Products are less likely to lend themselves to precise, objective evaluation in a service activity, while markets may not disclose quite so completely who the customers are and what they want. On occasion, too, it may be that none of this information is revealed at all.

In service organisations quality hinges partly on:

- what the organisation's objectives are
- how well they are met
- whether or not they conform with quality

The National Trust is an excellent example of such an organisation.

THE NATIONAL TRUST'S ACTIVITIES

The National Trust is the UK's largest owner of land and historic houses. Its activities are dispersed throughout England, Wales and Northern Ireland, and are principally concerned with the administration of property and the management of public access to most of it. The Trust has also some ancillary activities, such as the running of tearooms and shops, most of which are associated with major properties. Standards in its activities are similar throughout the country, and are high. In all of its activities, there is a certain 'style' to the National Trust.

There are perhaps four outstanding objectives facing the Trust:

- preservation of its properties for posterity
- achieving access to these by the public
- securing approval of, and meeting various needs of, other parties concerned with or affected by the Trust's affairs
- conducting its activities within its financial constraints (being organised as a charity, its financial options and limitations differ from those facing a commercial organisation)

None of these factors are independent; all are linked and there are some conflicting pressures: balances have to be struck.

Preservation and access

Preservation and access are at the heart of the Trust's values and objectives, and the balance between them is achieved in the light of long traditions and current realities. Founded in 1895, the Trust was intended to preserve open space and the right of access to it for the general public, with a particular emphasis on the needs of those from deprived urban areas. Yet even in those early days it seems that in fact preservation was seen as the prime function; there is a comment from 1895 that the Trust is only a *caretaker*. A formal statement on the issue came a generation later from John Bailey, Chairman of the Trust between 1923 and 1931. This established the principle – held to this day – that, if there is conflict between the two, preservation should always take precedence over access. The principle is simple in outline but in practice it is hard to work to, as it sets ill defined limits on the uses to which properties can be put and the financial returns that can be generated. The Benson Report of 1968 was to note perceptively that the Trust is not part of the tourist industry and that this makes its job, essentially conservation, all the more difficult.

But, though of secondary importance to preservation, access has also been a cherished value of the Trust – and never more so than at the present, with a growing public perception of the Trust's attractions and rising enthusiasm for participation in 'green issues'. Besides, the matter of access is related both to Trust income, at many locations, and to any drive to increase membership. Clearly there has to be a limit at a few locations, where numbers approach saturation levels, but this is a localised and relatively clear-cut problem. Much more widely seen and difficult to handle are some of the consequences of providing and encouraging access. For if a large fee-paying public is to be attracted, a measure of infrastructure must be provided to serve it. However well designed and unobtrusively sited, facilities such as car parks, made-up paths and lavatories start to change the nature of a property and take it away from the context and values which the Trust is also trying to preserve. Possibly imperceptible at first and of negligible proportions if access is open only to a few, the effects of this policy of substantial access, accompanied by a few limited commercial ventures, help to maintain the prominence given to the preservation issue today.

The several parties concerned with and affected by the National Trust

First and foremost among the National Trust's strategic stakeholders – the groups of interests affected or influenced by its actions – is the nation, or the national interest. This is laid down by statute and so has the great advantage of being clearly and widely recognised. Although working for the national interest, the Trust remains essentially independent of the state and the government. Several other groups are in a position of secondary importance to the nation but may nevertheless assume a critical value to the Trust. Some of these parties are:

• Potential donors of property and assets. The great majority of

Trust properties have been and are acquired through donations. Many donors continue to live in part of the donated property and are therefore very closely associated with the Trust's operations. Excellent relations, both formal and informal, between the Trust and its donors are essential.

- The Trust's members, a group that has grown substantially in recent years. The members provide a large proportion of the Trust's recurrent income. Having joined in increasing numbers for what the Trust offers and to support its values and policies, the members may be viewed as a force for stability.
- Customers and visitors to the Trust's properties. The dominant stakeholder by far in nearly all commercial organisations, customers are just one among several secondary stakeholders to the Trust. A major source of revenue, they are likely also, at many locations, to determine the success or otherwise of some of the Trust's policies.
- Political and minority pressure groups. Several pressure groups are represented by only very small numbers but are vocal, publicity-conscious, and thus are generally a rising force.
- Full-time and part-time employees. Currently the full-time payroll is around 2,200. Seasonal staff numbers are slightly greater than this, at around 3,000.
- Voluntary workers. Many people give voluntarily of their time, in widely varying amounts. The Trust estimates that some 20,000 each year help in some capacity or other. Of mutual benefit in nearly all cases, the relative importance of voluntary help was high when the Trust started but fell away later. In recent years it has grown in relative terms and substantially so in absolute terms.

Finance at the National Trust

The Trust's activities have to be run within the constraints of its finances. From its inception, the Trust aimed to work without public funds, so that it could retain the independence of its policies. Doubtless it would be a very different organisation if there was an overt link with the government: the culture would be altered and large numbers of donors and voluntary helpers would be discouraged from giving their help. There is always the chance that the Trust's benefits from various fiscal and legislative measures might be less numerous if its work should diverge radically from government views, but happily such a conflict has never yet arisen.

Financial independence there may be, but freedom of discretionary choice is constrained as many of the funds either are endowments or have been donated for specific purposes. Furthermore, the Trust is not a commercial organisation. Such limited ventures as it has – tearooms and shops – would doubtless be vastly greater if financial returns were to have the first priority. But they do not, they are most unlikely to and the balance of several compromises is influenced accordingly.

DEFINING QUALITY AT THE NATIONAL TRUST

How should the National Trust's results be judged against its objectives? Its conservation of buildings and the countryside are to a high standard, and one that is remarkably consistent throughout the country. There is a passion for authenticity, while radical conservation choices which might compromise future discretion tend to be avoided. Intrusions from infrastructure are minimal – and, indeed, sometimes improve a property. The Trust's management of public access is exemplary, and its ownership now brings many properties to the attention of a wider public than would otherwise be the case. Standards of maintenance, husbandry and preservation are widely known, and can provide an added attraction to the public. Widespread political support is enjoyed and there is consensus support, too, from members and the public. Yet the Trust remains remarkably sensitive to pressure groups and to various aims and objectives favouring minorities. Judge the Trust by what it is leaving for posterity, compare its activities with the almost identical functions performed by numerous local authorities, several government departments, museums and similar independent organisations both in this country and overseas, and nearly always the comparison is favourable to the Trust. Frequently, it is highly favourable.

However, some criticisms can be levelled at the Trust and many of these amount to arguments over the point at which compromises have been made. Thus it is possible to make impassioned cases for more access, for less, or for more commercial activity and infrastructure as well as for a large reduction. The view taken here is that the Trust's priorities are well chosen. There is also criticism which tends to overlook some of the Trust's objectives. This can be illustrated using comparisons between the Trust and the best of the private owners. Forget for a moment the situations where there is indifferent stewardship or a lack of funds, and compare the Trust with the best of owners, providing inspired, painstaking restoration and husbandry. In properties built originally for private occupation, with access intended to be for only a few, it can be possible to draw an unfavourable comparison for the Trust. A dedicated owner of adequate means may be able to add a degree of sympathy and personality which no organisation could match, but – and this is critical – such fortunate individuals do not face the compromises which the National Trust has to make.

Perhaps most important of all is a limitation that arises partly from the Trust's size and its consistent policies. Its work has to appeal widely, and can rarely take a path where there is a risk of controversy or any reduction of the options facing posterity. There is authenticity in its restoration, yet this must be tempered by a measure of conservatism. Cost, too, must curb innovation in an organisation with limited funds and many potential demands. Such effects are unlikely to be noticed by nearly all National Trust members and visitors but, for a minority of professionals in architecture, art and ecology, who make frequent trips to Trust properties, the results can seem bland and even uninspiring, and theirs is an informed and articulate opinion. Arguments may be raised which introduce subjective judgements and leave open certain questions of taste. Once again, though, the case for the Trust having quality may be re-established if we recall its need to balance its objectives.

HOW DOES THE NATIONAL TRUST ACHIEVE QUALITY?

Success for the Trust is not a foregone conclusion, although certainly it has many advantages. People give their time freely to it, but this is true of other charities as well, and the results can be mixed. The Trust has exceptional properties, fine works of art and outstanding areas of countryside, yet other organisations with notably more plentiful finances exhibit comparable items and employ a more corporate style. Let us look at some of the factors to which success may be attributed.

Strategy and the stability of the National Trust's policies

Policies have been remarkably stable at the National Trust. Much of its philosophy and strategy were established by its founders nearly a century ago, and most of the changes and additions since then have been relatively minor improvements, introduced either in the light of experience or as reactions to current conditions. For example, the standard of properties accepted has gradually risen. Small pieces of land were found to be unsatisfactory holdings over the longer term, so their minimum size was raised and other criteria made more stringent. Necessary endowments for properties have been increased, too. Furthermore, certain developments in earlier years led either to mistakes or to a pattern of use, which might have been acceptable at the time, but would not have been permitted later and would be unacceptable today. The solution here has generally been to keep a closer, more direct control of properties than was formerly considered necessary.

Some other important, reactive influences on strategy have come from the outstanding conservation needs of the day. The emphasis for acquisitions in the early days was on the preservation of the countryside and open space. This was to change as adverse economic circumstances made it difficult for existing owners to maintain large historic houses. In numerical terms, these have been delivered to the Trust in cycles, notably in the 1930s, in the years following World

War II and then, more recently, in the late 1970s. Today there are still difficulties here and there with historic houses, but for the most part they are safe. Instead the focus of fresh efforts has moved back to the countryside, where the threats have increased and are rising.

Policies at the Trust are an expression of the membership's wishes to the extent that, if a measure is wildly out of line with the majority view for long, something would be done about it. This background of consensus approval can be related to the political support the Trust has enjoyed from all sides of the House of Commons, and to the six major pieces of legislation in which it has been involved.

Today, it faces some very long strategic timespans; questions involving building preservation and woodlands have horizons of many decades, land is held in perpetuity, while endowments are calculated over 50 years. Among the nearer-term aims are to have the Trust increasingly open to the outside world and to its members. Education and the way the Trust relates to schoolchildren are to receive particular attention. Voluntary help is to be encouraged and the generation of additional sources of income investigated.

Organisation and management style

The National Trust's organisation is composed of a structure of committees and of an executive staff which has evolved over the years primarily to accommodate substantial growth. The current outline of the structures of the committees and the executive, their authorities, duties and reporting relationships followed from the recommendations of the Benson Report (1968), formalised by the National Trust Act (1971). However, as the Trust expanded in the following decade, a variety of informal changes were soon found to be necessary. In particular, the executive needed greater authority and managerial scope, and so ways were found of developing it. A review in 1983-4 by a working party under the chairmanship of Simon Hornby sought to recognise this process, extend it and impose it on the nominal structure (parts of which are covered by statute). Thus, by a process of altering the status of senior members of staff relative to the committees, the inclusion of some key executives as committee members, and the replacement of some of the smaller committees by expert panels, the Trust has arrived at its current structure.

Authority is nominally vested in Council, a committee of 52 members which meets four times a year. Half of Council is elected for three years in rotation by the membership. The Director-General heads the executive; subordinate to him are the full-time staff, just under 10 per cent of whom are at the head offices in London with the remainder working from the regions. Subordinate to Council are the committees, consisting of the executive committee, several committees for specialised functions (also based at head office) and the regional committees. Formerly the staff served the committees, but now there is a split of duties, functions and responsibilities. The executive committee is appointed by Council and consists of all the regional chairmen and another 12 or so independent members. Having delegated much authority to the executive committee, Council has in recent years assumed a role comparable to that of a body of trustees.

More authority now resides in the hands of the Trust's executive than in the past, yet still there might appear to be a danger of a damaging conflict of interests arising from the division of power within the committees. However, the structure is easy to defend, partly since it works and partly because the committees were a major reason for the early success of the Trust. By 1899 there was a Finance and General Purpose Committee and an Estates Committee was set up the next year. More were to follow. The formal methods which these adopted were sufficient to handle the growth of the Trust over several subsequent decades. Increasing size and complexity led to the appointment of some full-time specialists, notably land agents, after World War II but the limitations of a centralised structure were only to set in as late as the 1960s. The Benson Report recognised the limits of the central committees' managerial capacity and actions taken in the light of it both strengthened the committees and reduced their workload through extensive decentralisation.

Standards and the co-ordination of activities

Consistency in the Trust's activities throughout the country is achieved primarily through co-ordination from the centre. Another factor is that senior members of staff in the regions are appointed to the central specialist departments: historic buildings, finance, land agency, public relations and publicity, and enterprises. Periodically, staff are brought together from around the country for specialist conferences, and this helps to disseminate a common approach. Wide differences between regions might have been expected to arise from the financial constraints we have noted, but this effect is offset partly by the local allocation of income generated within the regions and partly through the distribution of funds received at the centre. These are disbursed on a basis related to need, so that there is scope for countering disparities. A baseline is set to represent what each region is trying to do, and then ways are examined whereby the line can be raised.

CONCLUSIONS

Today the Trust is able to bring to its broad objectives the wider participation of experts and others from outside through membership of its committees. It is an organisation with an unusually varied set of objectives which succeeds in attracting many able people, some of whom donate their time, and then channels this participation and energy towards its ends. Full-time staff are left to concentrate principally on managerial and executive duties, while the committees handle policy and some specialist functions. At a local level, the committees are invaluable in relating effectively to actual and potential donors of properties.

But the Trust's structure cannot necessarily be taken as a model by other non-profit-making organisations. Its objectives lead to some unusual requirements from its structure, while the cohesive effects of policies, recognised and overwhelmingly supported by staff and committee members alike, are considerable. Furthermore, the Trust is amazingly fortunate in the calibre of those who serve it and work a system which elsewhere might lead to divisions. However, as an example of quality in a service organisation, achieved substantially through participation, it is outstanding.

11

British Aerospace Airbus Division

BACKGROUND

British Aerospace Airbus Division is the part of British Aerospace's commercial division which handles work arising from the company's 20 per cent stake in Airbus Industrie. Around two-thirds of the Airbus Division's payroll of 9,000 is currently engaged on producing Airbus wingsets, and this proportion is rising. Of the division's other activities, the most notable is a maintenance contract for the US Air Force.

Public perceptions of Airbus Industrie differ widely and can have an effect on the generation of quality. On the Continent, Airbus Industrie is seen as an outstanding success story. Other government-assisted attempts to establish high-technology manufacturing activities may have had mixed results, but civil aircraft have fulfilled their promise. Projects which involve years of development have been brought to fruition, the products' quality has been second to none, the orders have followed and now Airbus Industrie is destined by the mid-1990s to become one of the largest – if not *the* largest – manufacturing businesses in Europe.

By contrast, in the USA Airbus Industrie is seen as an instrument of discriminatory trade policy. The Americans doubt if the only major competitor in the Western World for their own aircraft manufacturers, built up as it has been with the crucial help of public subsidies, could have arisen as a commercial venture. In Europe, however, such help is not seen as an unfair trade practice in view of the very substantial aid that US civil aviation had in its earlier years from high public expenditure, mostly for military purposes. Certainly, there is no simple answer to the question of who had the greater help from the public sector, the Americans or the Europeans.

In the UK, the public image of Airbus Industrie has been clouded by other criticisms which centre on its structure, profitability and managerial difficulties. Many of the problems have stemmed from the differing aims of its members and the way these aims have altered over time, so that agreements which once might have been acceptable to all are now no longer so. Airbus Industrie was formed by organisations in France, Germany and Spain whose funding and marketing relationships placed them effectively, if not in name, within their respective public sectors. There is room for argument over just how close or distant the relations with national governments were, but we can say that certainly none of the three founders had the corporate culture, aims and motives of a private-sector profit-making enterprise. Building up the business was more important than getting a return from it.

UK participation was initially as a subcontractor through Hawker Siddeley, whose aviation interests were later nationalised to form part of British Aerospace. Full membership of the consortium followed, but soon afterwards British Aerospace was privatised and started to apply some tougher criteria to its activities. The German partner has recently undergone a similar change of status, so the prospects are that Airbus will begin to adopt a more thorough-going commercial approach. In the meantime, however, the legacy of the past will take several years to eliminate and there are some working details which might tend to blunt the commercial pressures and motivation. All of these factors may affect quality.

THE DIVISION OF WORK AND THE RETURNS

Airbus Industrie is an organisation in which work and its associated financial returns are shared in proportion to members' interests. However, until historic losses are fully recovered by profits, members' returns are calculated in proportion to the accumulated losses they have carried. The total of losses is unknown and, in any case, the calculation depends on the definition of some accounting identities, but their effect is to place the rewards of current effort several years into the future. Clearly, this must affect attitudes within the consortium. However, even if the accumulated losses could be disregarded, commercial motivations would still be diminished since the returns to the partners for their current work are almost entirely cost-based. In layman's terms, you get back from Airbus Industrie what you spend, while any surplus is spread across the partners in proportion to their shares: 37.9 per cent to each of the French and German partners, 20 per cent to British Aerospace and 4.2 per cent to the Spanish partner. Thus, even for the two largest partners, only a minority of the marginal operating profit, following a greater effort, will flow back to the member making it.

The division of work is another cause which can lead to a divergence between the returns members get for similar efforts. Work is divided in proportion to members' stakes but, as the division is at an early stage in a project's life, it is based on cost forecasts rather than on actual figures. Budgets on large projects do not necessarily lead to variances, but experience proves that they almost invariably do. Besides, the nature of work around an aircraft differs, and it would be surprising if inflationary trends were identical between the different work areas. Even if work was perfectly divided at the outset, it would be unlikely to remain so. Adjustments can be introduced every time a new project is launched, but the opportunities for this are rare.

With this confused background for motivation, what happens to quality? One view is that, having enjoyed launching aid, the partners could have concentrated on the products and produced better quality. Such an argument tends to be invalidated, however, by the difficulty of finding other examples of subsidies leading to quality in public-sector corporations, let alone in a sector involving technical progress and very complicated products. Instead, the converse is likely to apply; that confused motivation will lead only to the detriment of costs, returns and quality. But, whatever the outcome, quality survives at Airbus Industrie despite these handicaps.

QUALITY IN CIVIL AIRCRAFT

How good is quality at Airbus Industrie? Does it produce the best machines in terms of design, engineering and finish? It is not hard to find that opinion. But defining quality differences between aircraft is not a simple issue. Certainly, Airbus has its strengths, but the competition is considerable and has its own strong points; one player is good at this, another is good at that. In particular, both of the major US competitors have had much more practice at selling and marketing, and it matters. Even with the best aircraft, there are so many aspects to quality that there will always be room for its improvement.

Another reason which complicates quality comparisons between aircraft manufacturers is that standards are set by the principal national authorities on a number of design parameters, such as safety provisions and airworthiness requirements; all producers have to meet these if their products are to be acceptable worldwide. The standards achieved have to be similar, and distinctions on these matters are of little consequence, so the scope for quality comparisons is narrowed. But that still leaves a large field. The influences on Airbus Industrie can be attributed to the central organisation, to the procedures and traditions of the partners, and to certain external factors which may have a differing impact between competitors.

QUALITY FROM THE AIRBUS INDUSTRIE ORGANISATION

Airbus Industrie *per se* produces nothing but has a central organisation with responsibilities, duties and functions to which its partners contribute, receiving certain services in return. For instance, the design definition is set centrally and the partners' contributions may lead to differences which have to be resolved. Bring four opinions to an issue and the outcome can be better or worse than if the question had been left to a single partner, depending on how the proceedings are managed. That Airbus succeeds through a common view in producing some outstanding designs and harmonising standards among the partners is therefore very much to its credit. Increasingly, quality is being promoted at this early stage by incorporating some of the implications of manufacturing engineering.

This central organisation also affects quality through being responsible for the final aircraft. It can and does come back to the partners for improvements and the elimination of defects. It carries out the production-acceptance checks and the flight test from the standpoint of a separate organisation to the production facilities, and this helps to establish broad standards.

One difficulty which could affect quality at Airbus Industrie, the geographical dispersion of production sources, is apparently shared by others. Modern aircraft development and construction have become such large projects that the US competitors source subassemblies and components at least as widely as Airbus does.

SOME OTHER EXTERNAL INFLUENCES ON QUALITY

While Airbus Industrie helps establish the principle of quality, most of the detail for its generation is left to the partners. Some of their methods vary, partly due to the different approaches their national authorities take. In the UK, the Civil Aviation Authority (CAA) has operated virtually from the start of commercial-aircraft manufacture and has made a valuable contribution to quality. As well as establishing the airworthiness requirements, the CAA also laid down some associated engineering standards – concerned rather more with production than with design – with which manufacturers had to comply. Constructors had to demonstrate that these standards had been met at various stages of manufacture. The CAA, among other things, carries out an audit of the business and looks at organisational procedures and practices.

Customers are another major force for quality. They all differ, and British Aerospace Airbus Division is placing an increasing emphasis on relating to them. Among its customers the US military provide a notably positive force for better quality: they are exacting and they go into great detail.

Competitors, too, have to be monitored carefully, as the state of the art on production methods and on several major operating ratios is set essentially by reference to the competitive environment. Inventory turnover, for example, on wingset production has risen steadily at British Aerospace in recent years and currently stands at about 2½ times. There is a possibility that conditions cannot be compared exactly between producers but, if the best inventory turnover appears to be four times, there is evidently scope for improvement within the limits of today's methods and capital equipment, so four times is the target for Airbus Division by 1991.

QUALITY AT BRITISH AEROSPACE AIRBUS DIVISION

External factors have an important role, but ultimately British Aerospace Airbus Division and the other partners rely mostly on their own pressures and traditions to generate quality. Professional engineering standards and pride in individual work have been very strong traditional forces for high quality at British Aerospace. The product plays a strong role here, as aircraft are inspiring, exciting products to be working on. They attract good people and help to bring the best out of them. Although personal attitudes towards work may have changed down the years, the sense of awareness is different and individual horizons and expectations have altered, yet still there is much pride in work and pressure for quality at an individual level.

The pattern of participation is influenced by the nature of union activity at plant level. Thus, although group working and quality circles have been introduced elsewhere in British Aerospace, this has not been the case in the Airbus Division. Part of the reason is that, in a heavily unionised environment, communication and participation cannot be changed easily in such a radical manner. Much communication is channelled through the unions, and the methods used have been developed in the light of local conditions.

Training has traditionally received a very great deal of attention at British Aerospace. There are many apprentices, typically around 250-300 in the Airbus Division as a whole, and their training programme is run internally. Higher up the organisation, all management goes through a management training system, for which a combination of internal and external courses is used, the proportion depending on the managerial level. Consideration of quality affects the content of courses, with stress being placed on topics such as customer orientation, the awareness of suppliers and what constitutes an affordable cost. However, these are essentially adjustments to what was already a substantial educational programme.

The effects which standards have in developing quality may vary between locations. Standards are partly a motivational influence intended to set quite specific pressures, but people can react to them differently. Obviously, efforts are made to find and select those who react positively, but this is not always possible.

The rise of quality assurance

Around 4 per cent of the manual workforce at British Aerospace Airbus Division is currently engaged on inspection functions of some type or other. About 15-20 years ago, quality managers were introduced progressively to replace the inspectors, whose numbers gradually fell. A rather different philosophy of product quality accompanied this change. Formerly, the aim was to produce engineering excellence but now the goal is excellent engineering, a concept requiring a broader view of an item's function and with a higher priority for costs and the complexities of production. Essentially, the need is for excellent engineering at an affordable cost. This can lead to fresh approaches to all activities, from design onwards. Interestingly, statistical quality-control methods do still have some applications, but not nearly so many as in mass-production flowline operations.

Differences between the Airbus partners are seen in their handling of suppliers. British Aerospace is well ahead in having an approved-firms system, with inspections every two years, while the other partners still place a much heavier emphasis on inspection. The approach and rigour used are similar to the CAA's quality approval of constructors, and the system is highly efficient when applied to large suppliers. Problems do, though, start to arise with smaller suppliers, for whom the vetting procedure is not necessarily faster, and for British Aerospace this has been exacerbated by the rise in the number of sources as output has expanded. Increasingly, producers with a proven record of high quality have come to be valued.

QUALITY THROUGH VOLUME IN BATCH PRODUCTION

Remarkably, perhaps, growth at British Aerospace has enhanced quality: rather than decline as output has risen it has, if anything, improved. The scale of the necessary investment, together with the associated planning, provide part of the answer as to why this should be so, while another factor has been the very close watch kept on quality. But these alone are not reason enough to explain the improvement. Instead, a phenomenon comes into play whereby long production runs can lead to better quality. On a very complicated item, such as a wing, a variety of alterations and improved methods become apparent which can only be introduced if a substantial production volume is in prospect. Very rarely are these amendments specifically aimed at better quality but, where any change is made, a house rule is that quality must either stay constant or improve. And so it is that, the longer the production run, the more changes are made and the greater the stream of likely quality improvements. Historically, British civil-aircraft production has nearly always been in very small runs, and the introduction of such a series of minor incremental changes could not be justified. The large orders for Airbus have made the difference.

TOTAL QUALITY AT BRITISH AEROSPACE

The last five years have seen the introduction of a total-quality programme at British Aerospace. An enhanced awareness of the value of quality and how it is generated has been accompanied by much greater readiness to question existing standards – to ask if things really are good enough. Quality costs, too, have received attention. Information on costs has to be re-examined to give a picture of where the money is being spent. Cost is ultimately the greater part of what quality is about in a situation where technical standards have always been high. Designs will evolve, materials will improve and there may be many minor increments waiting to be made to standards, but the principal effects of a total-quality drive will be seen through costs. Normally, too, for a commercial organisation, those effects will be reflected through profits.

12

Ford Motor Company

ROAD VEHICLES AND QUALITY

Quality has always been a major issue in motor manufacturing, by virtue of the nature and complexity of the processes involved, but at some times it has been of greater concern than at others. A complicated product has to be designed, specified and assembled, while suppliers have always been important. The proportions of components produced in-house and bought-in has varied, but the difficulties of ensuring that deliveries are made of appropriate components at the right time has always been a crucial operational issue. Customers have been discerning, prices and market positioning have needed careful attention and all of these pressures have affected quality. It might be only in recent years that the term 'quality' has become widely recognised as covering and influencing so much activity but, under whatever name, Ford has redoubled its emphasis on quality since the mid-1970s.

PRESSURES FOR BETTER QUALITY

This strategic change of direction towards a much greater concern for quality was not predictable from the historical record. Amazingly, too, in retrospect, it was not at the time widely spotted by outside observers. Financial results in the 1970s were satisfactory – indeed, very good in comparison with those of some competitors. Ford's quality and reliability also compared favourably with at least some other UK producers. The motor industry attracts much comment, yet the press had failed to address the issue of quality in a comprehensive sense for the sector as a whole. Such coverage as existed was typically concentrated on just one measure, such as reliability. There was even a tendency for national chauvinism over the product to obscure the underlying disparity between UK quality and standards elsewhere. Consequently, it was possible at the time to produce a study of the industry, based on press cuttings and a literature search, without mentioning quality at all.

The realisation that a radical quality improvement was needed at Ford was a triumph for the consensus viewpoint and for the strategic contributions which can come from a planning process. It arose principally from an analysis of the competitive situation and, in particular, of what all the other competitors were doing. Favourable comparison with a few of these was not enough if there was a huge disparity elsewhere, notably in Japan. Quite evidently, the Japanese were getting something right. Their output had risen at a high and continuous rate at a time when, from around 1960, the picture in the USA and Europe as a whole had been one of, at best, low growth.

A number of Ford managers visited Japan in the late 1970s and were profoundly shocked by what they found. The Japanese were far ahead on many, many matters – and not just those factors affecting quality. The various findings from these visits were collated and a presentation put together for internal purposes, titled *After Japan*. Clearly, Ford just had to improve.

Quality at Ford is what matters to the customer, and customers' needs alter. An additional cause for concern and a further stimulus for change was to come from a report commissioned from an economics consultancy in the early 1980s. This noted that the customers for cars were already a discriminating market, and forecast they would become even more demanding. Irrespective of the competitive position, therefore, the factors denoting quality to the customers were expected to become more stringent. Somehow, Ford had to respond to this situation.

Customer relations

One step taken by Ford to raise quality was to attempt to get closer to the customers, to find out what they wanted and thought and how the pattern of their requirements changed. Indeed, if there is one thing which other organisations can do to improve quality, both rapidly and effectively, it is to go out and identify their customers, talk to them, understand them and isolate their needs. The smaller the organisation, the easier this is likely to be, since it is closer to the customers to start with. A large company could be at a disadvantage in this respect, and just has to work harder at it.

Marketing and design cycle

At Ford, market information is put together by a design and marketing process which now works to a system known as 'Concept to Customer'. In effect, customers' needs are monitored as closely as possible and then related by a central group to the products. The notion of 'Concept to Customer' has been instrumental in moving activity to generate quality further towards the concept, influencing it, altering the design and so on. This has been accompanied by an attempt to take the quality effort away from final inspection to earlier stages in the production and design cycles. There is now a far greater emphasis on designing quality into the product.

Although the company is seeking to eliminate inspection carried out as a routine, production-related activity, inspection survives in the sense that all facets of quality are monitored. Thus samples are taken and checked in every conceivable way, while warranty costs are examined and compared with those of the competition. Different Ford locations are looked at, too, as all are supposed, insofar as they can be judged against each other, to be producing identical quality. The whole exercise is also performed from the opposite standpoint: what went right rather than what went wrong. All of these functions could be seen as inspection, but they can be distinguished from measures to verify specifications after manufacture and prior to the point of sale. Inspection, after all, aims for conformance to a specification, whereas Ford is constantly looking for product changes which are considered by the customer to be improvements.

Supplier relations

Suppliers are so important to Ford that it was realised from the outset that a quality-improvement programme would have to include them, too. Furthermore, Ford had to be the catalyst for change and the driving force for quality, as it was closer to the final customers than the suppliers would ever have to be. Ford expected to have to follow a more difficult path in its supplier relations than had the Japanese manufacturers. Many Japanese suppliers are allied to the assembly plants through the pattern of ownership and control, all of which could simplify the solutions to quality problems. As it was, Ford had to build up mutual trust, bring suppliers into the design process much earlier and, at the end of the exercise, award larger and longer contracts.

SPC and the production plan

Designs and specifications are reached through the application of techniques, and for every process there is a technique or method and a skill which works. Choosing the right one may be problematic, and errors may arise, but that is largely a technical question. Statistical Process Control might be seen as a technique, and certainly it is applied everywhere it can be at Ford, but in an increasing number of applications it is really just the theory behind the practice. Today, systems for manufacturing control tend to be built into the processes, control charts are superseded and SPC is used as merely one element of the theory behind the computerised practice. The extent of computerisation in operations is largely a question of the rate of capital investment; by the end of 1989 the number of computers used in connection with processes had more than tripled over the previous decade to total 587. (This figure excludes microcomputers and therefore understates the rise of computing ability.)

JIT techniques are employed at Ford in the sense that groups called JIT teams were used to investigate operational issues and problems and to come up with recommendations. JIT is mostly about inventory reduction and the putting together of a production plan, both subjects that have a long history and can be attacked in many ways. Somehow the 'JIT' label tends to be dropped at Ford as soon as techniques are actually being implemented.

Ford's outline production plan is triggered by final demand as it produces to order but, beyond that generalisation, it is a highly complicated procedure. The plan has always attempted to maximise the use of resources and to reduce costs of all kinds, not just inventory costs. Today it differs significantly from the past in using information technology and modern distribution methods; indeed, these have developed so far that the plan is dependent upon them and could not operate without them. Quality is affected by the plan and is obviously a priority. However, with several other objectives encouraging and conditioning the outcome, it may be questioned whether anything is done differently as a result of the closer concern for quality.

TRAINING

Training is central to the improvement of quality at Ford and, like quality itself, is driven by needs: what skills does the organisation require, what has it got and how is the difference to be made up? Essentially, these questions define the programme. There is a utilitarian character to it all; far too much 'nice to know' material is believed to be taught in other companies, and this is a practice that Ford tries to avoid. Instead, training to the trainees is a matter of what they have to do and whether they have the skills to do it. Both of these questions are affected by quality.

Appropriate training for quality is something which any Ford employee can master. Differences in ability and educational attainment there may be, but anyone can be taught what there is to be learned if he or she has the will to learn and to benefit from the experience. Trainee motivation and attitudes are of paramount importance in a training function.

Driving the suppliers' quality forward meant that they, too, had to undertake much training. Significantly, it did not start of its own accord. Training programmes are determined by needs, and Ford assessed these by requiring the buyer for each account to visit the suppliers and isolate them in every case. Ford then had to create the vast majority of the training material and the means of its provision. The organisation also encouraged and licensed a series of educational providers around the country, and on some topics even paid for the suppliers to have the training. A certain independence over compiling its training provision can be related to the prime origin of Ford's own quality; it is decided by the customer, and Ford has to do what appears to be necessary to respond to the market.

It was necessary to get the suppliers into a position where not only were they providing what was needed but Ford had confidence that they were doing so. Accordingly, it had to set up its own quality-assurance system, with emphasis on the particular provisions for the vehicle-manufacturing business. Assistance was given as required for the initial compliance, and thereafter the system and its standards have been maintained by a series of direct contacts and sample checks of products. Again, there is no set pattern to this activity: positions are investigated as often as is necessary.

ATTITUDES AND COMMITMENT

Perhaps the outstanding lesson for quality at Ford is that, while skills and techniques are needed to design and then produce something to a prescribed standard, commitment and constructive attitudes are absolutely essential if the customers are to be satisfied thoroughly and consistently. Everyone must *want* quality and be prepared to work together to get it. In an industrial setting, this means that group working has to be developed successfully. Groups have to interrelate in a cross-functional manner, and any structural features and departmental objectives which interfere must be adjusted to the common aims. Total quality is really about people working together as much as anything else. People have to be respected and trusted, and they have to work honestly with each other. This is where the Japanese motor manufacturers really score heavily. Yes, they have techniques and skills, but above all they recognise and value those attitudes supportive of quality.

13

Marks and Spencer PLC

Marks and Spencer's reputation for quality is legendary, even outside its principal trading sectors of clothing and food. It relies mainly on the standards in its stores and on its widely recognised policy of getting quality right in the first place – only then does it introduce questions of price and returns. Furthermore, Marks and Spencer is an organisation which has succeeded through quality. It is the UK's largest retailer, its margins are high and consistent relative to others in the sector and, consequently, it is financially strong. Since 1986, Marks and Spencer has been the only retailer in the world whose corporate paper carries a triple-A credit rating.

Trading and financial success for Marks and Spencer are completely associated with quality, and a reminder that this is the correct strategy for the group came in recent years from its activities in Canada. Expansion there started in 1975, proceeding largely through acquisitions, and early in the 1980s a situation developed in which the company temporarily overlooked quality. Market pressures and local traditions appeared to point towards trading down, so standards were allowed to drop. It proved to be a mistake, but it was corrected.

MARKS AND SPENCER'S VIEW OF QUALITY

To Marks and Spencer, quality is a relatively simple marketing concept: it is about pleasing the customer in every aspect of a product. First, you ask what the customer wants, or what he or she thinks is needed, and then you attempt to meet it. Sometimes Marks and Spencer is behind the market in this process, sometimes ahead. In foods, for example, the group has driven certain standards forward and led the market to expect and demand more exacting conditions. Its strategy of quality has also led away from volume groceries towards some specialised niche markets, in several of which it has the largest market share. Marks and Spencer's activities in food are recognisably different to the other major food retailers.

TRADITION AND CONSERVATISM

In some ways, Marks and Spencer's interpretation of quality has long been associated with a degree of conservatism. This is not the only approach to quality in retailing and one alternative is to place a greater emphasis on fashion. Thus in textiles, it has been unusual for Marks and Spencer to take a high risk policy with merchandise. This could be partly a consequence of its market share. With over 16 per cent of the entire UK clothing market, it has some very much higher shares of certain lines, which necessarily have to be served with classic middle-of-the-market styles. Nevertheless, there are competitors with a more aggressive policy towards fashion, who might seem more adventurous in comparison.

Perhaps more important than this, however, is the hint of conservatism introduced by the quality strategy itself, as pursued by Marks and Spencer, for quality improvement has been an incremental process. Over the company's history of more than a century, it has been continually looking to up-grade its performance and to get people to pay a little more for something which is very much better. It has been an evolutionary process in which progress has advanced by a series of small steps, building on previous achievements.

This is not in itself a conservative approach, but over the last generation it has been possible to identify competitors with a distinctly different style towards at least some aspects of retailing. Discarding something from what was there at the outset, bringing in the designers, pouring in a substantial and continuous stream of capital expenditure and introducing an innovative product range – that, in broad terms, has been an alternative strategy followed by several groups. Some of its followers may have had little to build on, several may have had a notably more volatile profits record than Marks and Spencer, but if these criticisms of competitors are disregarded, those who build on tradition can be left looking conservative.

TRADITION AND PERSONNEL POLICIES

An essential feature of quality at Marks and Spencer is that some of the aspects of its systems, procedures and culture which, with hindsight, might be associated with total quality programmes, appear to have been instigated long ago for other reasons. An ultimate concern to raise the effectiveness of the organisation's efforts might have been in the picture somewhere, but quality was probably not the prime objective. Examples of this are to be found in the staff welfare programme. The company records its former Chairmen, Simon Marks and Israel Sieff, finding in the early 1930s that some employees were actually going hungry, not because their wages were insufficient to support themselves but through being the sole source of income for their families. The solution was to provide meals and various other benefits, either free or at low cost to the employees, for which purpose a welfare department was started in 1934. Such a programme makes a great contribution to motivation and respect for individuals, which is an essential part of achieving staff commitment to quality, but it does appear to have been initiated for philanthropic reasons.

TAKING QUALITY TO THE SOURCES OF SUPPLY

In its early years, Marks and Spencer was reselling goods which it had obtained from wholesalers. This allowed discretion over price, presentation and service, while there were great gains to be made from operating through much larger and more efficient stores than had been previously commonplace. But quality gains were essentially limited so long as the same merchandise was available to other retailers and there was little influence over its design and production.

The watershed in Marks and Spencer's procurement policy, which paved the way for quality gains in later decades, came in the mid-1920s. Simon Marks and Israel Sieff had found that available goods were not exactly what they wanted. Consequently they broke with the historic buying procedure and started to design and specify products which manufacturers produced for them. The first supply contract of this nature was awarded to N. Corah in 1926. As goods obtained in this way were unique to Marks and Spencer, a house brand name became necessary. St Michael was devised and registered in 1928.

As this new approach to procurement expanded, it had to be formalised. Several specialist departments were set up: the Textile Laboratory in 1935, the Merchandise Department and the Design Department, both in 1936. Together, these helped to move the generation of product quality back from testing and inspection by Marks and Spencer to the production processes and incoming raw materials. However, it was to be many years before most of the results could be generated, due to the imposition of direct controls in wartime and in the post-war austerity period.

CODIFYING PROCEDURES

Another development, also started in the late 1920s, which was later to be of great significance, was the process of documenting procedures and standards, first for its own operations and then for its suppliers. These nevertheless established the principle of codifying measures, putting them into practice on a consistent basis and then monitoring the results.

These events of over half a century ago are still of great interest to total quality programmes, for they came at a time of great expansion for Marks and Spencer, the number of stores almost doubling in 15 years, reaching 239 by 1939. This compares with a total of 280 in the UK today, though extensions and developments have greatly raised the capacity of individual units. Yet despite the pressures of the time, it was possible to take measures which set the scene for quality a couple of decades later. Furthermore, the changes at Marks and Spencer were not made by a newly arrived chief executive, or someone from outside bringing a fresh insight. Simon Marks was a second-generation entrepreneur who had become a director in 1911 and Chairman in 1916, a decade before the company started to order its own designs.

GENERATING QUALITY TODAY AT MARKS AND SPENCER: PERSONNEL AND THE COMMUNITY

Today, quality at Marks and Spencer rests first and foremost with its staff and their attitudes. Quality pervades the entire organisation because staff are treated with trust and respect. With such a background, administrative procedures can be simplified and team-working is possible. High morale is reflected in the service received by the customers, and excellent communications within the company help to promote quality through its staff. A communications group airs concerns to a senior level before they become a problem, and there is an open-door policy, with a ceiling to personnel managers from the junior levels.

Consistent with this enlightened policy towards its personnel is Marks and Spencer's widespread community involvement. Substantial donations of funds and help are made to charitable causes, while recently a series of measures have been instigated to promote Green issues.

COMPETITORS' QUALITY

Quality is the main competitive factor for Marks and Spencer and competitive pressures are therefore an important influence. Competitors' quality and various other aspects of their performance are monitored continuously. Much of their merchandise is watched closely, with successful items being subjected to a meticulous analysis. In every possible detail, competitive conditions are examined for ways in which improvements can be introduced and for areas where particular effort is needed.

THE TECHNICAL DEPARTMENTS AND PRODUCT QUALITY

Some technical functions are carried out in the USA and Europe, but the dominant centre is at Head Office in London. There, the technical departments are central to the generation of product quality. With almost 700 technical staff, the design, marketing, merchandising and the analysis of products, materials, processes and competing products are carried out in closely related departments. These are primarily organised by product groups, corresponding to the main sections of a Marks and Spencer store, though certain functions, such as design trends and fabric performance, are separate. The physical location of these functions in one building and the consequent high standards of communication and information flow appear to be major contributors to the resulting quality.

Product quality at Marks and Spencer is based on the examination in great depth of almost every conceivable aspect of an item. Details and properties of a product, its manufacture and its raw materials are all investigated exhaustively. Following this analysis, any implications, recommendations and procedures are drawn up for use elsewhere which are then put into a form so that they can be understood and carried out consistently by whoever uses them. This is absolutely crucial. Material may have to be translated into a foreign language and must, almost invariably, be simplified to a level which can be followed by semi-skilled operatives. Particularly where a specification, standard, procedure, or test will be carried out by suppliers' personnel, who are unknown to Marks and Spencer, the matter must be related to the lowest grades to which it is likely to be entrusted, to ensure reliable and accurate work. Thus, on many aspects of product quality, implementation relies on a series of simple documents. To put them into effect, you have to be literate, numerate and possess just a dash of flair for practical issues, but that is all.

Relating product quality to those who will carry it out may be seen as a part of effective communication with those who are further up the production chain. Essentially, Marks and Spencer does whatever is necessary to promote communications with its suppliers and puts its information into a form which will be suitable for those who are contacted. The resulting dialogue is very much a two-way process, with Marks and Spencer in its turn receiving much information from the suppliers.

Another important way of establishing the confidence that a process will be carried out reliably, predictably and accurately is to reduce the cost of doing it. This may be illustrated by many of the tests which Marks and Spencer devises, develops and simplifies. Clearly, if a procedure is costly, it may not be performed with the stipulated frequency. Equipment is redesigned to lower its initial cost, but possibly more important is its simplification, so that its operation does not rely on highly paid personnel with significant technical education and experience.

THE USE OF PUBLISHED STANDARDS

Published standards are used wherever possible, but their coverage is not wide enough for all of Marks and Spencer's activities. There is also the criticism of much published material that it is pitched too high for some of the people who will put it into practice. The style and content of published standards tends to be aimed at managerial level as, doubtless, it has to be in the first instance, but all too often managers are not the people who have to work with the detail. Difficulties, misunderstandings and confusion can arise, but they can be overcome by simplifying and clarifying the published material.

A second difficulty for Marks and Spencer arises where a topic is handled without enough depth, or where available certification procedures in the sectors it is interested in are insufficiently exacting. Thus Marks and Spencer produces standards of its own and still operates a quality system for suppliers. This has to be specialised to textiles and must relate to everyone concerned, not just to managers. Suppliers are certified annually: Marks and Spencer maintains several certification centres for this purpose, two in the UK, two in Hong Kong and two in Europe, while three more are being developed, one in Europe and two in North America.

THE QUALITY MANAGEMENT TEAM

Aside from the technicalities of marketing, design, product specification and product quality, a measure of professionalism is needed in quality management. This is provided by a small group which consults in-house and to the suppliers on questions of quality. It is known as the Quality Management Team, and it holds workshops at the locations where they are needed.

QUALITY AT STORE LEVEL

There is still partial reliance on a checking system for incoming goods to maintain quality at the stores and occasionally returns have to be made. The principal mechanism for disclosing error and disappointment, however, is through a generous returned-goods policy, where details of customer dissatisfaction are carefully noted. Another source of corrective information is customer complaints, which currently run at around one thousand per week out of a weekly purchase transaction rate of 14 million. All of these are noted, logged, analysed and may be acted upon outright. Any trends or abnormal movements are always investigated and can lead to the withdrawal of a line of merchandise.

COMPETITION AND CONCENTRATION AMONG SUPPLIERS

There may be gains in quality to be made from working closely with suppliers, but doubts can be raised over whether competition is ultimately compromised. After all, if a supplier is encouraged to integrate its output to match the demands of a retail chain and elaborate quality procedures and systems are jointly built up, then the two organisations may continue to work together partly because they have done so in the past. An increasingly formidable hurdle could thereby be created which potential competitors have to surmount. Such a danger of reduced competition is countered by Marks and Spencer always being open to approaches from small, specialist producers. Quality may have to be achieved first by a prospective supplier to gain initial recognition but, once established, Marks and

Spencer will provide the support, if necessary, to develop a supplier's facilities to handle the quantities which are needed.

SOME REFLECTIONS ON THE CURRENT OUTLOOK

Marks and Spencer's route to quality is that of a very large company. Its structure, quality procedures and systems were established and developed over several decades and anyone attempting to emulate them would face a long programme too. It need not take quite as long as Marks and Spencer since, with a foregoing example, the way to quality should be easier to find and, in any case, the intervention of the war years distorted the time pattern. Nevertheless, the horizon would be likely to stretch well beyond a decade, for the problem in copying Marks and Spencer's example is not so much in deciding what to do, but in generating a scale of activity sufficient to support the resulting overhead, most notably that of the central technical departments.

Some of the problems of building an operation run on similar lines to Marks and Spencer may be illustrated from the group's overseas expansion. Internationalisation, indeed, is the great challenge facing the organisation today. The first overseas moves came in 1975 in Canada and France, since when expansion has been largely by acquisition in North America and by organic means in Europe. There is also an operation in Hong Kong.

There may have been some disappointments with this overseas programme, but the picture is mixed and it is not without some bright spots. Perhaps the most optimistic scene is in the USA, where the two major acquisitions were made in 1988. Operations are still being turned round, but the group philosophy is proving eminently exportable since the targets were chosen partly for their cultural compatibility with Marks and Spencer. There is still some way to go, however, as margins in the USA are only around half the level of those in the UK.

In Canada, the situation is still one of recovery after the earlier mistakes and operations return a small overall loss. The European story is of slow growth, with only 13 stores established after 15 years.

Cautious penetration is coupled with margins rather lower than in the UK, despite having one Paris store selling 'more per square meter than any other department store in France'. This all points to a significantly higher cost base for Europe than in the UK. Thus the scale of enterprise in Europe, which is really only that of a medium-sized organisation, is likely to be more difficult to run profitably with Marks and Spencer's systems than the much larger UK operation.

The progressive development of overseas facilities to support the Marks and Spencer quality system is proceeding and substantial operations growth will be needed to justify them. The latest innovation for expansion in Europe is not to work alone with organic growth but to use the joint-venture, 50:50 basis, with the so-called franchise store, in places such as Norway, Hungary and Spain. It is evidently a formula which permits much faster market penetration, but it also poses some fresh problems for quality, particularly where it brings an association with manufacturing, as in Spain. Certainly, the group has an encouraging record for meeting such a challenge.

Bibliography

Benson Report on the National Trust, The, London, The National Trust, 1968

Berger, R. W., and Shores, D. L. (editors), *Quality Circles: Selected Readings*, New York, Dekker, 1986

Box, G. E. P., 'R. A. Fisher Memorial Lecture 1988', reprinted in *Industrial Quality and Productivity with Statistical Methods*, London, Royal Society, 1989

Collard, R., *Total Quality Success Through People*, London, IPM, 1989

Crosby, P. B., *Quality is Free*, New York, McGraw-Hill, 1979

Crosby, P. B., *Quality without Tears*, New York, McGraw-Hill, 1984

Dale, B. G., and Lees, J., *The Development of Quality Circle Programmes*, Sheffield, Manpower Services Commission, 1986

Deming, W. E., *Out of the Crisis*, Cambridge, Cambridge University Press, 1982

Fedden, R., *The National Trust Past and Present*, London, Jonathan Cape, 1974

Feigenbaum, A. V., *Total Quality Control* (3rd edition), New York, McGraw-Hill, 1983

Groocock, J. M., *The Chain of Quality*, New York, Wiley, 1986

Gunter, B., 'A Perspective on the Taguchi Method', reprinted in Chase, R. L. (ed), *Total Quality Management*, Kempston, IFS Publications, 1987

Halpin, J. F., *Zero Defects*, New York, McGraw-Hill, 1966

Ishikawa, K., *What is Total Quality Control the Japanese Way?*, New Jersey, Prentice Hall, 1985

Juran, J. M., and Gryna, F. M., *Juran's Quality Control Handbook* (4th edition), New York, McGraw-Hill, 1988

Lorenz, C., *The Design Dimension*, Oxford, Blackwell, 1986

Morrison, S. J., 'SQC is Not Enough', *The Statistician*, vol 36, no 5, 1987

Oakland, J. S., *Statistical Process Control*, London, Heinemann, 1986

Oakland, J. S., *Total Quality Management*, Oxford, Heinemann, 1989

Pearson, E. S., *The Application of Statistical Methods to Industrial Standardisation and Quality Control* (BS600), London, BSI, 1935

Peters, T., and Austin, N., *A Passion for Excellence*, London, Collins, 1985

Pilditch, J., *Winning Ways* (2nd edition), London, Mercury Business Books, 1989

Quality Systems (BS5750), London, BSI, 1987

Report of the Hornby Working Party, London, National Trust, 1984

Shewhart, W. A., *Economic Control of Quality of Manufactured Product*, Princeton (New Jersey), Van Nostrand, 1931

Shingo, S., *Zero Quality Control: Source Inspection and the Poka-Yoke System*, Stamford, Productivity Press, 1986

Storey, D. J., 'Quality Control Procedures in Small Businesses', reprinted in *Industrial Quality and Productivity with Statistical Methods*, London, Royal Society, 1989

Taguchi, G., *Introduction to Quality Engineering*, New York, Asian Productivity Organisation, 1986

Ughanwa, D. O., and Baker, M. J., *The Role of Design in International Competitiveness*, London, Routledge, 1989

Voss, C., and Clutterbuck, D., *Just in Time: A Global Status Report*, Kempston, IFS Publications, 1989

Index